The American Way

The American Way

BY DEXTER PERKINS

University Professor Emeritus
at Cornell University

Cornell Paperbacks

Cornell University Press

Ithaca and London

First published 1957 by Cornell University Press.
Published in the United Kingdom by Cornell University Press Ltd.,
2-4 Brook Street, London W1Y 1AA.

First printing, Great Seal Books, 1959
Second printing 1963
Third printing, Cornell Paperbacks, 1966
Fourth printing 1977

International Standard Book Number 0-8014-9017-0
Library of Congress Catalogue Card Number 59-10009
Printed in the United States of America

Prefatory Note

THE essays in this little volume are based on lectures given at Cornell University in my capacity as John L. Senior Professor in American Civilization. The friendly reception that they received in Ithaca has encouraged me to put them in published form. They are brief but, I hope, suggestive comments on some aspects of American history. More than this I do not claim for them.

DEXTER PERKINS

Cornell University
Ithaca, New York
February 1957

Contents

The American Way

Conservatism in America

ONE of the pleasant intellectual pursuits of the contemporary era consists in the redefinition of familiar terms, especially the terms "conservative" and "liberal." I by no means intend to disparage this activity; instead, in this essay and the one following I mean to have a hand in it. But there is in it an unresolved element. Both of the words that I have just mentioned are essentially subjective terms; what seems conservatism to one man seems rank reaction to another; and what is liberalism to one man is dangerous radicalism to his neighbor. Try as we may to divest these words of the emotional aura that surrounds them, we shall be obliged to confess that there is something about them that defies analysis. Yet this is no reason whatever for leaving the field to those who are least precise; in particular Professor Clinton Rossiter has performed a real service in attempting to give substantial and exact content to the term "conservative." If we are not to be dominated by words, if they are to be our instruments and not our masters, we must always be looking for their deepest meaning; and the words "liberal" and "conservative" are amongst the most frequently used and the most significant in our political vocabulary.

Perhaps the most sharply etched and satisfying description of the points of view that they represent is that of William Edward Hartpole Lecky, written more than seventy-five years ago. The only imprecision about it lies in the fact that Lecky used the word "radicalism" as a substitute for "liberalism." But we shall do no violence to his thought if we substitute the latter for the former, and, with this substitution, as an introduction to what follows, I quote from his *The History of England in the Eighteenth Century:*

The distinctions between content and hope, between caution and confidence, between the imagination that throws a halo of reverent association around the past and that which opens out brilliant vistas of improvement in the future, between the possible dangers of change and that which sees most keenly the defects of existing institutions and the vast additions that may be made to human well-being, form in all classes of men opposite biases. . . . The one side rests chiefly on the great truth that one of the first conditions of good government is essential stability, and on the extreme danger of a nation's cutting itself off from the traditions of its past, denuding its government of all moral support, and perpetually tampering with the main pillars of the state. The other side rests chiefly on the no less certain truths that Government is an organic thing, that it must be capable of growing, expanding, and adapting itself to new conditions of thought or of society; that it is subject to grave diseases, which can only be arrested by a constant vigilance, and that its attributes and functions are susceptible of almost an infinite variety and extension with the new and various developments of national life. The one side represents the statical, the other the dynamical element in politics. Each can claim for itself a natural affinity to some of the highest qualities of mind and character, and each, perhaps, owes quite as much of its strength to mental and moral disease. Stupidity is naturally conservative. The large classes, who are blindly wedded to routine and are simply incapable of understanding or appreciating new ideas, or the exigencies of changed circumstances, or the conditions of a reformed society, find their natural place in the conservative ranks. Folly, on the other hand, is naturally radical. To this side belongs the cast of mind which, having no sense of the infinite complexity and interdependence of political problems, of the part which habit, association, and tradition play in every healthy political organism, and of the multifarious remote and indirect consequences of every institution, is prepared with a light heart and a reckless hand to recast the whole framework of the Constitution in the interest of speculation or experiment. The colossal weight of national selfishness gravitates naturally to conservatism. That party rallies round its banner the great multitude who, having made their position, desire merely to keep things as they are; who are prepared to subordinate their whole policy to the maintenance of class privileges; who look with cold hearts and apathetic minds on the vast mass of remediable misery and injustice around them, who have never made a serious effort, or perhaps conceived a serious desire, to leave the world in any respect a better place than they found it. . . . On the other hand, the acrid humors and more turbulent passions of society flow strongly in the radical direction.

Envy, which hates every privilege or dignity it does not share, is intensely democratic, and disordered ambitions and dishonest adventurers find their natural place in the party of progress and change.

This quotation, brilliant as it is, is no more than a starting point; and, in applying the generalizations which it contains, Lecky, of course, had in mind the British political scene. I propose in this essay, having set the stage with this quotation, to examine conservatism in its American context, with a view to discovering what we really mean by it and in what sense it has been useful in the development of American political life.

But, perhaps, before we begin, we should clear the ground by indicating what conservatism does *not* mean in America. In the first place, it does not mean reaction. Reaction is an excellent word for the politicians in an election year. But, broadly speaking, if we were to equate conservatism with reaction, we should have a difficult time finding a place for it in the history of American politics. For reaction means going back to something that existed before. It means nullifying what has been already accomplished. It would be reactionary, for example, in the literal sense of the word, if the suffrage, once widened, were again restricted; it would be reactionary if, in the economic sphere, measures of control once imposed were removed. It would be reactionary, in the social sphere, if, once having recognized our duty to the unemployed, we repealed the statutes which provide the means for discharging that duty. The action could certainly be taken. But it is much more typical of the American political method to stop and digest reform rather than to overturn it. To take the most modern and the most striking example, the New Deal program of the Roosevelt era has withstood remarkably well the advent to power of those who criticized it. What is true of the New Deal is true of earlier eras. The administrations of Theodore Roosevelt led to regulation of the railroads and to attempts to put down monopoly. The impulse that led to these changes was exhausted by the end of the second administration of Woodrow Wilson; but the railroads continued to be regulated, and there were a number of antimonopoly suits even in the administration of Calvin Coolidge. There is in American politics a constant and healthy tendency toward the center. If the pendulum does swing, it swings in a rather gentle manner. We should reserve such a word as reaction for much more violent oscillations.

In the second place, it would be doing equal injustice to the conservative to describe him as a stand-patter. Immobility is a thing hard to be attained under any circumstances, but the conservative does not necessarily seek to attain it. He may, on the contrary, be interested in measures which, as he believes, will increase the general atmosphere of stability and make less likely the violent assaults upon the existing order which, by temperament, he is likely to dread. He may wish to see improved administration and greater governmental efficiency. He may desire to see legislation repealed which, in his view, has been unsuccessful in practice or which operates ineffectively in terms of the social and economic order. He is not bound by the laws of his nature to be unequivocally attached to the *status quo*.

In the third place, it would be wrong, I think, to equate conservatism with individual selfishness. The instinct of helpfulness can be expressed in many ways, and in ways that have no connection with a change in the social or political order. There is a wide field in this world for the exercise of the impulse of charity and public benevolence, and one of the most conservative communities that I know is also one of the most generous in responding to the call for public giving. Indeed, in some cases the very attachment of the conservative to the existing order may make him willing to take appropriate measures to see that its injustices are not left to fester and that its economic inequalities are not permitted to become so deep as to arouse the spirit of social and political revolt.

Finally, as to what conservatism is not, I must dissent, and dissent emphatically, from the point of view put forward by Professor Russell Kirk that conservatism is the necessary product, or at any rate the essential product, of the religious spirit. It is true that there is a sense in which religion may give support to conservatism. If one is preoccupied with the blessed hope of the world to come, if one regards one's state on this earth as transitory, preliminary to something far better, then it is easy to be patient under the slings and arrows of outrageous fortune and to feel that the amelioration of the human lot is of secondary importance to the worship of God and the observance of religious forms. But it is by no means true that the religious spirit always expresses itself in this way, and the whole history of the United States demonstrates the contrary. There is scarcely a great movement of reform in the hundred and seventy-five years of our national existence that does not owe something to organized religion. The most conspicuous example is no doubt the antislavery movement. But there are others, and I shall wish to deal with them in the next essay. It is sufficient to observe here that there is no inevitable connection between the devout man and the conservative. The maxims of Christianity may make for the calm acceptance of the *status quo*. They may make for the precise opposite, for a deep and religious-minded discontent with the order that exists. To equate religion with conservatism is to see religion itself in narrow terms and to read one's own creed into the Scriptures.

We have seen, then, that there are a number of things that conservatism is not. What are its essential characteristics? What are the elements in the conservative point of view?

At the head of the list, in my judgment, is to be put a not altogether sanguine view of human nature. The conservative temperament is disposed to believe that man is a good deal lower than the angels. It is disposed to give substantial recognition to the presence of evil in the world and to accept the fact that sin and selfishness are pretty much ineradicable. The conservative, in this regard, may not believe with Gibbon that history is little more than the record of the crimes, follies, and misfortunes of mankind, but he is well aware of the pitiable weakness of human nature. The record of the past is full of noble deeds, but it does not go far to confirm the belief that man is constantly rising to new heights of wisdom and virtue. Skepticism as to the human material, recognition of the fact that the achievement of today is sometimes the failure of tomorrow, the unhappy maxim that the more things change the more they remain the same, these are among the constituent elements of the conservative point of view. The conservative may well say with Marcus Aurelius that a man of forty years, if he have a grain of sense, having seen this sameness, has seen all. Perhaps his is an exaggerated view; perhaps it takes too little account of hope and too much account of disillusionment; perhaps the judgment herein expressed ought to be qualified or modified; but the fact remains that too many dreams have faded, too many reforms have failed, too many happy prophecies have gone unfulfilled not to give to doubt and caution a part in the vision of the future.

Because the conservative sees these things, because he recognizes the limitation of the human animal, he will, as a rule, have only a limited faith in the rule of the masses. True, in America it is necessary to give at least lip service to the democratic principle. The politician running for office must, in all but the rarest instances, make obeisance to Demos. He cannot deny the validity of the general principle of popular government. And, to say truth, he rarely wishes to do so. But if he is a conservative, he would, almost invariably, hedge that government with restrictions, he would limit its powers, he would at least find ways to prevent the impulse of the moment from dominating the political scene. He would argue, in all probability, that, while it might be possible in the long run to put one's faith in democracy, it was quite another thing to give to a transient majority the right to "tamper," in Lecky's phrase, "with the main pillars of the state." He might and sometimes does describe himself as a republican rather than as a democrat.

In the same way, and for the same general reasons, he would be far from sure that government could make over the social pattern or cure the dominant social evils. He would, as a rule, insist on the natural social, intellectual, and economic inequalities of every human association. He would not expect too much from efforts to redistribute property, or to raise the ignorant to the level of the instructed, or to break down the barriers that separate one group in a given society from another. I do not want to carry this point too far. It would be absurd to say that in America conservatives believe in a caste system. The whole experience of the past belies any such belief. One of the great conservatives of the early part of the nineteenth century was Timothy Dwight, the famous president of Yale. There can be no question of how we would classify him. He was in a sense the prince of Tories. But in that remarkable poem of his called *Greenfield Hill*, we find expressed precisely the "shirt-sleeves to shirt-sleeves" philosophy that is recurrent in American thought. The idea of the frozen society is not characteristic of this country. But some recognition of intellectual and moral and economic inequality is perfectly compatible with the American point of view. That such inequalities exist, that they have existed, and that they will continue to exist, despite the efforts of legislators and statesmen, is an assumption on which the conservative will usually stand. His conception of government is not that of an agency of social change. He thinks of the machinery of the state rather as a preservative than an originating force. He is not necessarily a little-government or a weak-government man. When we invoke the powers of the state, it makes a very considerable difference to all of us whose ox is gored. It may well be necessary at a given time to bring authority to bear, not to alter but to protect the existing order. Power may be invoked as much to withstand, as to promote, social change. To use power for the latter object may well seem to the conservative a hazardous and perhaps an unfruitful adventure.

It is a little difficult to state precisely what are the characteristic opinions of the conservative on foreign affairs. There is certainly no reason why the conservative should turn out to be a jingo. War is a monstrous interruption of the normal way of life; it may very easily end in the disruption of the existing order; it bears hard on the economy; it is the antithesis to the principle of order to which the Tory mind is usually attached. The American business classes, which are usually conservative, have been rather more than ordinarily conspicuous in their interest in peace. The strident nationalism that one connects with such a figure as Senator McCarthy is, therefore, by no means characteristic of the right as a whole and, as a matter of fact, it seems to be connected more closely with a certain social status than with any precise political philosophy. On the other hand, conservatism in the field of foreign policy will rest upon certain fundamental assumptions. It will take as its guide not sentiment but the national interest, which, however difficult to define (and it is *very* difficult to define), is something different from a diffusely benevolent attitude toward the world at large. It will assume, more certainly than will liberalism (though not necessarily in contradiction to it), that physical power is an essential constituent in the conduct of foreign affairs and that there are times when the threat or the use of such power is essential. It will seek immediate goals rather than long-range objectives.

But let us turn from this analysis of what may properly be described as the conservative point of view to an examination of the central question as to the services of conservatism in American life. In doing this, we shall have to make value judgments that do not command universal assent, for we shall have to affirm that certain policies which we regard as conservative have been on the whole desirable from the point of view of the public weal. We will not reach a consensus on this matter; but perhaps we can come near enough to one to make the discussion worth while. And we can, in a measure, objectify our conclusions by taking the viewpoint that, where a given position has met the test of time, it has vindicated itself from the standpoint of the common good.

Take, for example, the question of distrust of the powers of government. In the period of the Revolution, a period in which there was a drift to the left, there was a strong tendency to draw up constitutions which placed great power in the hands of the legislatures, provided for frequent elections, and segmented the authority of the executive. This was done in the name of democracy and on the theory that government ought to be close to the people. But this way of looking at the problem was not at all characteristic of the conservatives who played the leading role in framing the Constitution of the United States or of later generations who were to modify the constitutions of the various states. In the case of the national government, the whole framework betrayed distrust of what Gouverneur Morris described as an "excess of democracy." The term of the House of Representatives was made two years, the term of the Senate six, and the elections to the latter were so arranged that only a third of the senators were changed in any two-year period. The President was given a veto over legislation, a veto rarely conceded to the state governors under the early state constitutions. And, above all else, there was erected a system of federal courts with the power of review and, as it turned out, the power to declare both state and federal statutes unconstitutional. Every one of the devices I have just mentioned is an example of the conservative temperament. Every one of them is based on the hypothesis that there must be some kind of check on the ebullience of popular legislatures; every one of them implies that it is not the judgment of the moment but the reflective judgment of a longer period that ought to be the determinative force in government. And with this view I should be inclined to agree.

In the same way the Constitution calls for the creation of a strong executive. The so-called liberals of the eighteenth century feared the concentration of power as dangerous to liberty. But the framers of our fundamental document thought differently. They were impressed not only with the dangers that flow from the popular mood; they were impressed, too, with the peril that comes from the undue diffusion of power. They saw, more clearly than the libertarians, the necessity for providing a government that was strong enough to deal with its problems.

Their example has in the long run been followed more and more in the government of the states. There are, it is true, wide variations in the numerous states of the Union. But, whereas governors used to be elected for one or two years (they were elected for one year in Massachusetts well into the twentieth century), they are now frequently elected for four. Whereas they used to be compelled to run on a ticket which also carried the names of candidates for attorney general, controller, treasurer, and perhaps many other offices, they are now in many of the states permitted to appoint the principal administrative officers. Whereas in the early state constitutions they were often denied the veto, they now have the veto in almost every state of the Union. There is a tendency also to elect state legislatures for longer terms, and, to cite an example, the state of New York not so long ago amended its constitution to make this possible. In other words, the point of view of those who might have been called liberals in the early days of the history of the United States has been discarded, and the point of view of the conservatives has been accepted.

There are other ways in which we may identify some of the more desirable developments of our governmental system with conservatism. The rise of the masses to power, so dramatically illustrated by the election of 1828 and the ascendancy of Andrew Jackson, brought with it an extension and justification of the spoils system in politics. Men argued that the work of running the government was "after all," as President Harding was later to express it, "a very simple thing" and that it was therefore logical to give everybody or anybody a crack at it. This point of view is very properly outmoded. But the clamor for a change, for civil service reform, can hardly be said to have come from the left. It came again and again from staunch conservatives, from such men as Thomas A. Jenckes, George William Curtis, and Grover Cleveland. Indeed, civil service reform has never been a movement to arouse great popular enthusiasm. The very proper demand for better standards of administration has again and again come from the right.

Or, take again the problem of city government. The mismanagement of the affairs of the great cities of the country has been one of the blots upon the American political record. But the movement for the improvement of municipal standards has come about the hard way, and it has often been sponsored by conservatives while many of the rank and file of the voters have held aloof.

On one other question which involves the scope of governmental power, conservatives have often been on the side of sound principle. Those who take the Tory view toward politics will both welcome power and distrust it. They will be equally hostile to anarchy and to tyranny. And, because they are hostile to the latter, men whom most of us would describe as conservatives have often been amongst the defenders of that fundamental document, the American Bill of Rights. I know of no more remarkable illustration of this fact than the career of Charles Evans Hughes. In his general attitude toward government Hughes was certainly not of the left. But no man in both his personal and judicial career stood out more staunchly for the fundamentals of the American Constitution and for the protection of the minority against the attacks of the mob. When, for example, in one of the most ill-advised acts of the time, the members of the New York State legislature expelled five members of the Socialist party who had been legally elected in the City of New York, it was Hughes who excoriated their act in a brilliant and cogent public statement and who persuaded both the state and city bar associations to take action condemning the expulsion. On the bench, time and again, Hughes defended the unfortunate against the abuses of popular judgment. In the unhappy case of Leo Frank, accused of murder under the laws of the state of Georgia and tried under circumstances which strongly suggest the pressure of popular passion, Hughes as a judge insisted upon a new trial and upon fair procedure. In cases involving religious liberty he was again and again found defending the right of dissent against majority action. In cases involving radicalism he stood again and again for a square deal for the radical. Nor is Hughes unique in this regard. Such a man as Seth Richardson, the head of the Loyalty Review Board appointed by President Truman, was a thorough conservative whose conservatism meant, among other things, attachment to orderly process and a fair deal for those under popular condemnation.

I turn from a consideration of conservatism in its relation to governmental power to some consideration of conservatism in its relation to the social order.

The conservative, as I have said, is in the main not much dissatisfied with that order. He does not have to believe that it is perfect. But he is not convinced that it needs substantial alteration. Is he right or is he wrong? It has been very easy for American historians to place the principal emphasis on change and reform in the evolution of the United States. No one knows better than the historian that things do happen, that no society is likely to be static, and that the evils of the social framework demand to be remedied. But, in taking this point of view, as it seems to me, less than justice is often done to the American business class, which in general is no great lover of change. The reason for this is that many of us fail to appreciate the immense value of the man who operates the economic machine, who has to make the

hard day-to-day decisions from which the college professor is frequently exempt, who has somehow or other
to organize the vast economic apparatus on which we
depend for our present satisfaction and for our future
hope. It would be foolish to assume that the business
classes speak with the voice of God. It would be foolish
to assume that a government completely dominated by
them would be a desirable government to have. It would
be foolish to contend that there have not been times when
business groups have been blind to the signs of the time
and resistant to inevitable change. But to say all this is not
to say that they do not perform a distinct social service
or to deny that the wise conduct of affairs requires that
their place in society be recognized and their interests
taken into account. Perhaps this is clearer today than it
has been for some time. For the sharpest alternatives to
the present economic system are communism and democratic socialism. The case against communism does not
need to be argued. But what is striking is today that socialism is becoming more and more discredited as an
answer to the ills of humanity. I use the word in its literal
sense, that is, to signify the ownership and operation of
the means of production by the state. While the case for
governmental controls remains strong (and of this I shall
have something to say in my next essay), the argument
for nationalization has grown constantly weaker. In
practice, nationalization of railways, or coal mines, or
trucking services has by no means turned out to be a
panacea, and in many of the countries of western Europe
today there is a distinct reaction against the thesis that

industry ought directly to be managed by the state. In terms of actual success, moreover, our own society has shown itself to be more than equal to any other in the world. The empirical test seems to demonstrate that in our faith in free enterprise (qualified free enterprise, if you will) we have been amply justified by the result.

In regard to this whole problem, the conservative sees an aspect of the problem that is not always clear to the men on his left. It is well that there should be voices raised in any community in behalf of a more equal—or a more equitable—division of the goods of this world. But you cannot begin to talk about dividing the pie until you have the pie to divide. The conservative will ask the proper questions about the means of increasing productivity because he realizes this essential fact. He may fail to ask the question as to whether the makers of the pie are each of them rewarded according to some rough conception of their respective contribution to the result. But the one question needs to be asked as well as the other.

In recognizing inequality of reward and in asserting, as he probably will, that inequality of status is inevitable, the conservative is merely saying what the gentlemen of the left have been in due course forced to recognize. The experience of Communist Russia, the most radical of all societies in its origins and in its assumptions, amply illustrates this fact.

But let us turn from these general observations to the lessons of experience in both the domestic and foreign field. Is it not the case that the conservatives have often been right, right from the empirical point of view, right from the angle of what actually happened? It was conservatives, as we have already indicated, who framed the Constitution of the United States. They saw what their opponents did not see, that it was necessary to construct a stronger government than existed at the time to promote development at home and to enforce respect abroad. Not all of them were by any means disinterested. Not all of them were by any means 100 per cent right. But on the great essentials they saw clearly. Furthermore, when the national government was set up, they knew how to give it solidity and force. By the funding of the national debt and the assumption of the state debts they attached large classes to the "New Roof." And in the founding of the Bank of the United States and in taking an interest in manufactures they were promoting a type of society which in the long run was to raise the United States out of provincialism into large-scale power.

Or take the struggle of Andrew Jackson and the Bank. There were unsavory features about the Second Bank of the United States. There was an unpleasant side to its president, Nicholas Biddle, despite the aura of culture that surrounded him. There was a possible case against the concentration of power in the hands of a private institution which could influence the economic course of events throughout the nation. All this can be conceded. But on one fundamental matter the conservatives who inveighed against Old Hickory in the Bank war were fundamentally correct. The nation needed to control its credit mechanism, and the Bank provided a means of control. With regard to this central problem time may be said to have vindicated the opponents of the President.

Let us look next at the Compromise of 1850. The more extreme antislavery men deprecated this give-and-take on the question of slavery. It was conservatives such as Daniel Webster who put their whole weight behind some adjustment of the interests and passions of the North and the South. In the judgment of many competent historians today this was a service to the Union. Had the breach between the two sections come in 1850 the North would have been far weaker than it was a decade later when a network of railroads covered the country and cemented East and West and when the industrial life of the nation was much further advanced. In postponing the struggle, the compromisers have been in no small measure vindicated by time.

It is a difficult matter these days to discuss the reconstruction period that followed on the Civil War. The country, except for a part of the South in terms of persons and of geography, is more aware than it has ever been before of the moral necessity of giving to our Negro population the fullest recognition of their right to be treated as full citizens of the republic. But even when this is granted, it may still be argued that the conservatives of the 1860's had a strong case when they opposed the extension of the suffrage to the freemen so soon after the war. They could say with some reason that at least a minimum of educational and economic advancement ought to precede the grant of the franchise; and, while this argument would not receive universal acceptance, it is impossible, even today, to deny that the attempt to impose on the southern states, partly by military occupation, what they were not prepared freely to concede, ended in reaction and the unhappy freezing of the politics of the South into one-party rule. The attempt to enfranchise the Negro was a practical failure, as we know. The South evaded by devious legal means the prescriptions of the federal Constitution, and the memory of federal coercion furnished a fertile field for the demagogue and the enemy of reconciliation between the sections. Reconstruction was by no means the ghastly failure that the historians of the Dunning school made it out to be; but the purposes of the reconstructionists were thwarted, and the conservatives who resisted their policies might well claim that those policies were a failure.

One of the most interesting cases in which the conservatives may well have been right was on the issue of free silver raised in its most acute form in the election of 1896. I do not wish to be misunderstood on this point. The passions of the campaign of that year far exceeded the bounds of reason. It is not likely that the adoption of the silver standard at the ratio of sixteen to one would have brought the republic down in ruins. We have seen enough of monetary manipulation at home and abroad in the twentieth century not to take too melodramatic a view of these expedients. But the chances are that the victory of Mr. Bryan would have had a very bad effect on the confidence of the business classes and would have checked the recovery that had already set in after the panic of 1893. Moreover, we can say with confidence that the free silver remedy proved to be quite unnecessary. The opening of new gold mines and the cyanogen process of gold refining produced such a flood of this precious metal as to induce a rising price movement which made the resort to silver superfluous. At a time when the primacy of the money markets of the world still rested with Great Britain, it was better to have recovery come about in this way than by a change in the monetary medium. This is not to say that in the election of 1896 all the arguments, if one surveyed the total field of national policy, were on one side. There have been few elections of which this could be said. It is merely to say that on an important issue the conservatives may very well have been right.

Or, take a still more striking case. One of the reforms of the second decade of the twentieth century was national prohibition. That those who supported this cause were sincere, that they were right in tracing many social and personal evils to the misuse of alcohol, is not to be denied. But the remedy they proposed proved not only ineffective but positively harmful. It is by this time perfectly clear that the Eighteenth Amendment did not prevent the manufacture and sale of intoxicating liquors, that it did not in any important way solve the social problem connected with inebriety, and that, in addition to this, it introduced a new and fertile source of corruption into the body politic. Those conservatives who rightly insisted on the futility of sumptuary laws of this character and who predicted from the outset that the remedy was worse than the disease were vindicated by the event.

The repeal of the amendment in 1933 is the answer of history as to the validity of the "experiment noble in purpose," in Mr. Hoover's words, that was imposed upon the nation in 1919.

I venture to add one more illustration from the field of domestic policy as to the value of the conservative point of view. Our society is, on the whole, an extremely sound one. As it functions today, it represents a healthy balance of interests, a competition of countervailing forces, as Professor J. Kenneth Galbraith has put it, which tends to prevent the abuse of power by any one group in the community and which gives a useful stability to the economic order which is by no means incompatible with vigorous growth. But, as no one has pointed out with more cogency than Professor Galbraith himself, the operation of these countervailing forces can be put out of whack by inflation. Resistance to inflation is, on the whole, the formula of conservatives. It is they who insist, perhaps sometimes a little too dogmatically and rigidly, upon the necessity of a balanced budget; it is they who interest themselves in those administrative and technical reforms which, if wisely chosen and applied, effect useful and proper economies. The men of the left, who put the accent on acts of benevolence and nourish a more intense zeal for human betterment, are, on the contrary, often blind to fiscal problems.

This matter is so important that I venture to turn away from American illustrations for the moment to say a word about the current situation in Great Britain. As these words are written, the British are engaged in a bitter struggle to maintain and increase their hold on world markets. Their prosperity depends upon this. To achieve their end they must prevent wages and prices from rising sharply. They must, in the opinion of many, put up with some measure of unemployment as a necessàry means of arresting the inflationary pressure. It is by no chance that it is the *conservative* party that is directing its efforts to these ends. This is the kind of problem that conservatives may deal with best.

But let us turn from questions of domestic policy to questions of foreign policy. And here again we shall see that we have much to record from the point of view of the contribution of the American conservative. Let us recall again, at the outset, that the conservative men (and most of them were conservative) who framed the Constitution of the United States had as one of their purposes to erect a government that would be adequate to protect the interests of the nation in the field of foreign affairs. They had before them the deplorable record of the government under the Articles of Confederation, and they resolved to do something about it. They so ordered their new mechanism as to provide for a control of foreign affairs sufficiently centralized to provide for effective action; they gave to the President sufficient power to conduct the public business in the foreign field without too much difficulty. Moreover, these same conservatives had not been long in office before a serious problem arose. The French Revolution created a deep division in American opinion. Men of good will and optimistic temperament, men who remembered with a tinge of sentiment the aid of the French in the American Revolution and with a tinge of resentment the "tyranny" of Britain were well disposed toward the new republic and tended to wish to shape foreign policy accordingly. On the other hand, the Federalists, the conservatives, if you will, saw a different set of facts. They saw that American trade was largely with Britain; they saw that an understanding with the greatest of maritime powers was of more value than any connection with France; and, although there were many grievances against the former mother country and although the temptation to reprisals was strong, they chose to support the idea of a mission to London. This mission, discharged by John Jay, brought about a settlement, a settlement far from ideal, of the outstanding questions between the two countries, and it would be my judgment (perhaps the judgment of most historians of diplomacy) that the solution was a wise one. The demand for retaliation against Great Britain rested largely on emotional grounds; the desire for understanding on hard-headed realism.

There have been other occasions when the country has been well served in the field of foreign affairs by men of the right. The liquidation of a whole variety of controversies between the United States and Great Britain by Daniel Webster in the Webster-Ashburton treaty of 1842 is one of them. It may be, as Professor Bemis had contended, that in the matter of the Maine boundary, one of the matters settled in this treaty, Webster gave away more than he ought; but, if one looks at the arrangement as a whole, it removed a series of questions from the field of controversy and avoided what might have been an increasingly dangerous growth of tension. It was Webster again, along with Calhoun, who in 1846 sharply criticized President Polk's ridiculous demand for the whole of Oregon ("fifty-four forty or fight") and virtually compelled the President to come to a reasonable compromise (one in fact that gave the United States somewhat more than it may have been entitled to) on the line of forty-nine degrees.

Or look for a moment at the period immediately after the Civil War. It was another conservative Secretary of State, Hamilton Fish, who restrained President Grant from the visionary enterprise of the annexation of the Dominican Republic, with its accompanying prospect of keeping in power there an unscrupulous and unsavory dictator. It was Fish, too, who persuaded the President not to recognize the belligerency of the insurgents in Cuba in 1870 and whose steady hand prevented a serious flare-up when the Spaniards seized an illegally American vessel, the *Virginius*, in 1873, executed some of the crew, and detained the passengers. Of course, to a certain type of nationalist, none of these efforts to maintain peace will seem very laudable; but they seem to me, at any rate, to have corresponded with the long-run interests of the United States.

Nor, as we reach the twentieth century, can we withhold praise from a great Secretary of State who was in his dominant tone conservative. Charles Evans Hughes would be regarded by most of the specialists in the field of diplomatic history as one of the greatest, possibly the greatest, secretary of the twentieth century. He brought to an end for a period of almost a decade the serious tension that existed between the United States and Japan; he contributed, and contributed vitally, to the partial clarification of the vexed questions of German reparations; he did something to set under way what was later to be called the good-neighbor policy; he clarified American thought on the subject of the Monroe Doctrine. There were, as it seems to me, some areas in which he acted unwisely; but the record as a whole is a record which, with due regard to the mutability of human affairs, was in its time and place an excellent one.

Or take another conservative, Arthur Vandenberg. It was he who did yeoman service in connection with the Marshall Plan, which did so much to restore the economy of Europe and to bring back to prosperity that distracted continent; it was he who sponsored the resolution out of which grew the North Atlantic Treaty and the organization which followed on it; it was he who, in spite of his partisan leanings and prominent position in the opposition party, set the example of that kind of bipartisanship which has brought to the United States some of its greatest diplomatic successes in the postwar era.

Now in all that I have been saying on this subject I want to make it clear that some scholars may well disagree with some of the judgments that I have expressed. There might, conceivably, be debate also as to whether some of the instances of wise action that I have mentioned have not been sponsored by those who would call themselves liberals as well as by those who call themselves conservatives. This latter point I am free to admit. The line that separates the moderate conservative from the cautious liberal is never a very definite one. But the main thesis that I have been expressing is, I think, sound, that is, that those of a conservative cast of mind have often made an important contribution to American life and to the welfare of the republic.

There is one thing, however, that conservatives lack. That is glow. Their sense of human weakness, their understanding of the difficulties that stand in the way of alteration of the current order, their appreciation of existing values, all militate against a truly ardent desire to make the world a better place. Conservatives, at their worst, may lapse into complacent satisfaction with things as they are. For the great measures of improvement that characterize the history of the United States we must usually look to those of a somewhat different temperament. What that temperament is, and how it expresses itself, we shall discover when we examine American liberalism.

Liberalism in America

WHEN I was an undergraduate at Harvard, there was a course in Semitic literature given by Professor Crawford Howell Toy and patronized by the less intellectually energetic of the undergraduate body. On one occasion he put on the examination this question: "Name the countries on the other side of Jordan." And one gilded youth, who was obviously not equipped with a sufficient knowledge of the geography of the Holy Land but who, it must be admitted, possessed a ready wit, took his pen and wrote, "It depends on which side of the river you are standing." Having, in the preceding essay, attempted to enter into some understanding of the place of the conservative in American life, I am now going to cross Jordan and see if I can depict with at least equal sympathy the point of view of the liberal.

Let us begin, as we began before, by distinguishing liberalism from radicalism just as we distinguished conservatism from reaction. There are such things as radicals and revolutionaries, just as there are such people as reactionaries. And Europe knows them well. The irreconcilable parties in France—the Communists on the one hand, the ridiculous collection of malcontents known as the Poujadists on the other—these are what the extreme terms radical and reactionary connote. The monarchists in Italy and again the Communists, these are outside the framework of conservatism or liberalism in any true sense of the word. Indeed, in many countries less fortunate than our own, government has to be carried on through parliamentary bodies in which some groups are hostile to the very existence of the regime which is in power. But in this happy country of ours such a phenomenon does not occur, and, as I shall show in my next essay, radicalism has found a very insecure foothold. When this country wants to move, it is liberalism, not radicalism, that dictates the course.

The essence of liberalism lies in the positive desire for the improvement of the social, political, economic, and international order. One of the dictionary definitions of liberal is "generous." This seems to me to lie at the heart of the matter and forms the starting point for our discussion. A humane interest in his fellow man, a firm conviction that there is the possibility of a better world than actually exists, a recognition of the inequalities, injustices, and selfishnesses that are so evident, these things furnish the aliment for the liberal. He wishes to go forward toward a better world. He does not put the accent on violence, for violence outrages his deep sense of the dignity of man. He does not envisage a millennium, for he knows that the human problem is of the ages and that the struggle for human betterment is never-ending.

He asks nothing more than that we should continually strive, that we should view the obvious difficulties in the way as obstacles to be overcome rather than as the basis for frustration or resignation.

Such a point of view toward life is based on certain broad conceptions that we must now examine. The first of these, as I see it, is optimism. This optimism is very far from utopianism, at least for the average American. The dream of the perfect world is not characteristic of American political thought, or of American leaders in either the intellectual or the political field. A kind of tentativeness always broods over American politics, and with it goes a sense of something incomplete, of challenges still to be met, of jobs still to be done. There is a strong feeling that the future may be better than the past —not perfect, but better. There is a desire to be up and doing, and a faith that labor will bring forth rewards. This faith is confirmed by history; for the majestic pageant of the American past shows a nation that has been constantly growing, that has been raising its standard of living, improving the lot of the ordinary man, opening wider and more varied opportunities to its expanding population. In such an atmosphere liberalism is bound to thrive.

Coincident with this optimism goes faith in the democratic process itself. There must be times when even the most cheerful of us are not altogether satisfied with popular government. Occasionally the demagogue, the successful demagogue, makes us doubt of the wisdom and sobriety of the common man. In the fifties the country

[31]

went through an experience of this kind with Senator McCarthy. Unscrupulous, violent, with no respect for truth, and still less for the integrity of the individual personality, for a few years the senator from Wisconsin terrorized governmental agencies, intimidated witnesses, and wielded a potent influence in Congress. Nor is this situation the only example of the kind of thing that leads men to denigrate the democratic process. The conduct of political campaigns hardly presents most men at their best. Exaggeration, name-calling, the blatant appeal to special interests, and ignorant prejudices, these are far too common accompaniments of the electoral struggle. Even the best men fall a victim to temptation. Wendell Willkie was a fine American. Yet, after the election of 1940, he could say, as if it were a matter for humor, that his prediction that Roosevelt would bring us into war within sixty days of election was "just politics." Ex-President Eisenhower is in many ways a noble figure. But in the campaign of 1952 he could leave the name of a great American, George Marshall, out of a pre-election speech in deference to the senator from Wisconsin. Franklin Roosevelt was a great president, but he equivocated shamelessly in his contest for the presidency in 1940. Examples of this kind of thing could be indefinitely extended.

And yet American liberals continue to believe deeply in democracy. Why is this? For one thing, because the product is so much better than the process. Look at the details of government, and they are frequently a just matter of criticism, and sometimes positively repellent.

But look at the record, as Al Smith used to say, and the record is impressive. After all, the broad story is a success story, not a story of weakness or failure. In the face of the achievements of the last hundred and seventy-five years, why *not* believe in American democracy?

But there is much more to the matter than this. American liberalism can make out a much better case for democratic government than this purely pragmatic one. It can make out a case that is, in the true sense of the word, spiritual. For what is the essence of the democratic process? Someone has said that popular government rested upon the conception of counting heads instead of breaking them. Is it nobler to count heads than to break them? Certainly. For in the process of counting some intellectual and moral elements inevitably enter. A political campaign may be very far from an appeal to pure reason, but rational processes are there, just the same. A political campaign may be very far from an ideal way of reaching a decision, but at least it does not rest upon violence and naked force. What, indeed, is the story of man, if it is not the slow attempt to substitute for the ruthlessness of nature some elements of the ethical and the rational? And what form of government so clearly emphasizes these elements as does democracy, since it assumes that *all* men are capable of the appeal to conscience and to reason. Perhaps the faith implied here is excessive, but perhaps also faith may be the mainspring of useful action.

There is another way, however, in which the American liberal will look at the democratic process. He will start from the central assumption that no kind of class government is good government. There is no element in the community that is sufficiently enlightened to judge the interest of all. Not the well-to-do, not even the successful and self-made well-to-do, for they may easily be warped by their own comfort or by their own success in judging the affairs of others. Not the college professors or any other intelligentsia, since they may easily suffer from the kind of intellectual arrogance that is very far removed from the needs of humanity. Not the government administrator, since he may become a slave to the machine which he efficiently conducts. Not the workingman, for his view may be limited by his ambitions and his interests. The only government that can function with justice to all is the government that represents the interests of all, the government that stands for all of us. The processes by which this government operates will not be ideal. But all views will be felt and expressed, and the attempt to harmonize these views, so the liberal would say, is as near as one is likely to come to some kind of abstract justice. A government resting upon these principles will, as Jefferson once said, be the strongest government on earth. It will be strong because it gives everyone an opportunity to speak; it will be strong because its conclusions will represent a consensus of thought and feeling; it will be strong because its very processes make for accommodation, compromise, and understanding.

It is to be granted that, in taking this view, the liberal rests his case upon a kind of transcendental belief in the common man. It is this belief that Lincoln expressed so touchingly in the words of his first inaugural: "Why should there not be a patient faith in the ultimate wisdom of the people? Is there any better or equal hope in the world?" It is this faith that Jefferson expressed in another way when in his first inaugural, speaking of other types of government, he said, "It has been said that man cannot govern himself. Has he then found angels to govern him?" The faith may at times be shaken; it does not require that at all times and at all places men shall act reasonably and in the true spirit of self-government; but the great historic record seems to confirm it, at least so far as the United States is concerned.

In this connection let me digress for a moment on one of my favorite themes. It is popular today to denigrate the processes of American diplomacy, and those who do so often put the blame on democracy itself. But is the record so gloomy as we are sometimes led to suppose? The great governments that fought against the democracies in 1914–1918 are long since in ruins; and so, too, are the autocratic regimes of Hitler and Mussolini and Tojo. Where now are the conquerors of the early forties? Hitler died in the flaming ruins of the bunker in Berlin; Mussolini was done to death by a mob; Tojo saw the structure that he had erected utterly collapse. And what of Stalin, the Kremlin autocrat? We have learned, not from his external enemies or bitter doctrinal foes but from the lips of those who fawned upon him, that he not only blundered badly at home but that he committed the most egregious errors in the field of foreign policy, grossly miscalculated the intentions of the German Reich, willfully and needlessly antagonized the states of the West, alienated the people and the government of Yugoslavia, failed to understand the nature of the great revolution that was taking place in China. Why then should we be so modest about our own form of government? Why should we not say—can we not say—that the grossest errors of the last two decades have been made not by the democratic peoples but by those who have committed themselves to totalitarian regimes? In the long run, the liberal believes the best wisdom is to be found in the collectivity, not because any member of the collectivity is himself as wise or as well-informed or as disinterested as some notable individuals may be but because the reconciliation of the wills, the aspirations, and the interests of all, even the prejudicies of all, provides a more solid, enduring basis of action than the will, the aspirations of any individual or class.

A second fundamental conception of contemporary American liberalism is that the power of government is to be used, and can be effectively used, to promote human happiness. This has not, it is true, always been the case. The liberalism of Thomas Jefferson—and there was no truer liberal—was closely attached to the notion that that government is best that governs least. In a simple agrarian society which had no very difficult or complex problems (as measured by the standards of today), there was something to be said for this idea. At a time when government had been associated historically, as it had been down to the end of the eighteenth century, with the rule of a class or with the rule of a despot, it was natural enough that government should be distrusted and that the emphasis should be put on freedom from external controls. But even in this early period, as we shall see later, when faced with a concrete problem which troubled their consciences or touched their aspirations, the liberals of the late eighteenth and early nineteenth century were ready enough to turn to governmental action. Their doctrine was one thing; their actual conduct something else.

When I say that liberalism implies the use of the power of the state to cure or moderate social evils, I do not mean that the liberal is by any means an all-out advocate of governmental power. He cannot be. The kind of gigantism that characterizes such a regime as that of Hitler, or that of the rulers in the Kremlin, is far removed from liberalism. And in one phase of affairs, the liberal will, even today, look askance at interference with the individual. His democratic creed ties him firmly to freedom of speech, freedom of the press, freedom of worship. His optimistic view of human nature makes him believe that when a question can be widely and fully discussed the chances are greatly increased that it will be settled right. His sense of the dignity of the individual, of any individual, makes him recoil at the idea of coercion of other men's minds. His warmth toward others makes him tolerant of those who disagree with him and reluctant to call them to governmental account.

Finally, to complete this brief analysis of liberalism on the theoretical side, liberalism in the United States has been historically connected with a strong desire for the promotion of international understanding. The liberal cannot be a narrow nationalist. He cannot be a jingo. He cannot be a subscriber to the doctrine, the nefarious doctrine, that the affairs of states are a matter to be regulated by physical force alone and that moral conceptions have nothing to do with the matter. It is not necessary, of course, that he should be one of those naïve people that cannot understand that power has a substantial place in world affairs. He need not be a believer in an immediate millennium. But he will tend to believe that the range of international co-operation can be substantially increased; that a wise conception of self-interest is not only compatible with, but tied to, collaboration with other peoples; that extensive as is the rule of force, there are other factors to be considered in foreign policy; and that it is as erroneous to ignore these factors as it is to brush aside the necessity for armies and navies and air forces in the present disordered world. His internationalism will be a judicious internationalism, not something fashioned out of dreams or concerned with a search for Utopia.

There is one more general observation to be made before we get down to cases and try to examine the record of American liberalism. I think it is fair to say that American liberalism, as I have defined it, has grown more powerful with time. It has grown more powerful because the urbanization of American life has inevitably widened the field of social action. At the same time, the Western world is faced with competition from another system which, whatever its cruelties, its violation of individual personality, and its ineptitudes, is yet based upon the idea of the amelioration of the lot of the ordinary man. The temper of the times demands that more and more consideration be given to the lot of the disadvantaged and of the unfortunate; and whatever the limitations of socialism or communism, their doctrines have stirred men's consciences and made for greater sensitiveness to human suffering and to gross social inequalities.

It is the same in the international field. There was a time when what has come to be known as isolationism was rational policy for the United States. But that time has passed. The gospel of "going it alone," expressed by General Douglas MacArthur more than a decade ago, is out of date. The times require that we co-operate with other nations for the maintenance of international peace and of our own security. The immense industrial growth of the United States means that we must look for expanding markets and seek external sources of raw materials. The horrors of modern war and the prospect of mutual annihilation which rises before us place the emphasis on measures of international collaboration and adjustment, however slow the process may be. Most of us realize today that the time has passed when a narrow kind of national egotism is prudent policy. Most of us have come to see that American foreign affairs must be conducted in a larger spirit than was necessary a half a century ago.

And now, having defined American liberalism and having ventured to assume that it is a permanent element and a growing one in American life, it becomes necessary to ask what are its historic roots and what are its actual manifestations in the life of the nation.

Liberalism, as we have already hinted, is based upon an optimistic view of the human experience. There is no country in which this optimistic view has flourished more continuously than in the United States. It has flourished here for several reasons. After all, coming to America meant a chance to rise in the world. Here was a society untrammeled by feudal traditions; here was land to be had for the asking; here was opportunity in the large sense of the term. The conditions of American life naturally fostered a cheerful view of the future.

But this belief in the future might not have been enough to nurture the spirit of liberalism if it had not been combined with other factors. The spirit of "getting on" might well have been a selfish spirit. What was needed was something more. And that something was found in the *Zeitgeist* of the eighteenth century, the century in which America really began to grow and in which it won its independence. This was the age of rationalism, the age in which men came to believe more deeply than ever before, as Carl Becker has so brilliantly shown in his *The Heavenly City of the Eighteenth-Century Philosophers*, that by the exercise of reason man could infinitely improve his status and the social order in which he lived and moved. The faith in progress that was characteristic of the era entered deeply into the American character. It molded the thought of many generations. And it gave encouragement and sustenance to the notion that, by taking thought, man could create a world in which humane men and women would delight to live.

But the rationalism of the eighteenth century was only one expression of the spirit of amelioration. For reasons that are not altogether clear, the religious life of America has always had in it a strong infusion of that kind of practical altruism on which liberalism feeds. It is not true (I repeat what I have written in an earlier essay) that religion and conservatism are identified. Almost every liberal movement in American history owes much to the churches. This was the case with the antislavery movement; it was the case with the peace movement; it was the case with the movement for social reform at the end of the nineteenth century. It is by no coincidence that American politicians, when fighting for liberal policies, often couched their appeals in religious language. We may doubt the wisdom of William Jennings Bryan's campaign for free silver in 1896, but if for the moment we think of it as he thought of it, as a crusade on the part of the masses, we shall understand what he meant when he said at the Chicago convention, "You shall not crucify mankind upon a cross of gold." We may or may not thrill to the Progressive movement which Theodore Roosevelt headed in 1912, but if we recognize this movement as one for social improvement we shall comprehend why he said at that time, "We stand at Armageddon and we battle for the Lord."

To say that the conditions of American life, freedom of opportunity, the rationalism of the eighteenth century, and the meliorative spirit of the Christian churches have formed the spirit of liberalism in the United States is not to say, of course, that that spirit has always been dominant. There is a rhythm in our history which has never been more suggestively described than in an article written by Professor A. M. Schlesinger for the *Yale Review* in December 1939 entitled "Tides in American Politics" and recently reprinted. Professor Schlesinger in this article pointed out the oscillations of American politics and drew up a little calendar from 1765 down to 1939 of the alternating waves of liberalism and conservatism. He comes to the conclusion that the average length of liberal eras is about sixteen years. I am not sure that I can accept this generalization, except in a very rough way. But the very fact that such a calendar can be made up is itself significant. It demonstrates that Americans have not only an instinct for change but an instinct for digesting change and that it is a pretty good thing to say of any people. There is moderation in American liberalism, as there is moderation in American conservatism.

There is one other generalization to be made about the nature of American liberalism that seems to me of some importance. It would be a mistake, I think, to believe that it is inevitably connected with depression eras and that periods of prosperity are inevitably conservative. The depression of 1837, a very long and deep one, produced no profound social stirrings in the body politic. The prosperity of the 1850's was a period in which the anti-slavery agitation became more and more intense. The long period of gloom in the seventies, 1873 to 1878, was not characterized by any fruitful movement of social amelioration. The prosperous period of the Taft years, on the other hand, produced a remarkable outburst of reformism in the movement known as Progressivism. Of course there are examples to be cited on the other side. The depression of 1893 produced a real movement of social unrest, and the depression of 1929 ushered in the highly constructive period of the New Deal. The problem of oscillation between liberalism and conservatism is too subtle to be solved by a simple formula.

Let us look now at the practical expression of American liberalism, and let us begin with the period of the American Revolution. In general, the Revolution was a movement for independence rather than a movement for sweeping domestic reform. But there were various steps that looked to some kind of change—the liberals would have called it progress in connection with the existing order. One of these was the abolition of primogeniture, the principle by which the eldest male child succeeds to the whole inheritance in land. In many states this principle applied at the time of the Revolution. It is true a man could devise his estate by will in some different fashion, and we must not make too much of the idea. Still, the acceptance of the concept made for concentration of economic goods, and those who opposed it were thinking in terms of the wider distribution of property. They were thinking, in other words, in terms of social democracy. They were thinking of the kind of society in which the benefits are widely diffused. And by 1789 they had had their way in every one of the states, and primogeniture had disappeared.

Take another matter. At the time of the Revolution established churches existed in many of the colonies. That is, the mass of the people were taxed to support some particular religious denomination. And this principle of favoritism toward some special sect existed not only in the South but also in northern states such as Connecticut and Massachusetts. Of course it ran counter to the fundamental principle that religious belief is an intimately personal matter and that no man ought to be called upon to contribute to a religious group in whose tenets he does not believe. In most of the states disestablishment took place in the period we are discussing, and in this, as in the struggle over primogeniture, Thomas Jefferson played an important part. It is a curious fact that the last relics of establishment were to be found in Massachusetts, where they were not abolished till 1833.

The antislavery movement attained new significance at the time of the Revolution. In the course of the war, or immediately after the war, most of the northern states abolished slavery, either out of hand or, like New York, by a system of gradual emancipation. And what was perhaps fully as important for the future, the famous Northwest Ordinance of 1787, which provided for the organization of the area north of the Ohio and west of the Appalachians as far as the Mississippi, contained the fundamental provision that slavery should not exist in any of this territory.

There was also, in the period which we are considering, a notable extension of the suffrage. Most of the thirteen colonies had property qualifications, both for voting and for holding office, the latter often much higher than the former. Nowhere was there genuine universal suffrage, even for males. But in the years following 1776 substantial changes were made. Vermont, which came into the Union in 1791, had universal manhood suffrage. Pennsylvania came very near it. And there was a general tendency toward the liberalization of the qualifications for voting, and one which was destined to gain ground as time went by.

It may be convenient, while we are considering the question of the suffrage, to pursue the matter beyond the Revolutionary period. For it is of the essence of the liberal point of view that there should be the very widest representation of individuals and of interests. It is not necessary to be doctrinaire on this point. In a country where there is a general opportunity for education, there seems to be nothing illiberal, for example, about a literacy test. But it *is* illiberal to restrict the voting privilege in such a way that all economic or social groups are not represented and given a free opportunity to express their views. It is strange, in retrospect, to see how very far from acceptable this principle was at the beginning of the nineteenth century. A favorite maxim of the conservatives was that those who own the country ought to govern it. There could be no clearer definition of oligarchy as opposed to democracy than this. Yet it was not till 1826, and only after a bitter political struggle, that the state of New York accepted the principle of universal manhood suffrage, and the triumph of the principle throughout the Union did not come until after the Civil War.

I am not speaking here of the enfranchisement of the Negro. This is an issue of importance, of course, today. And there can be no question of the manner in which the liberal will answer it. The possession of the right to vote is essential to the protection of the civil rights and of the economic interests of every class. It is no less essential to the Negro than to any other group. It can be argued, as we have seen, that to enfranchise a mass of illiterate freemen in 1867 was decidedly premature. But to insist upon the right of the Negro to vote under modern conditions cannot by any stretch of the imagination be so considered. We have not yet lived up to the principles of liberalism in this regard.

One of the great battles over the suffrage concerned the right of women to vote. The first place where women could vote (except in local elections) was in the territory of Wyoming in 1868. It took years before any other part of the Union followed Wyoming's example. But by 1893 Colorado had accepted the idea, and other western states followed. In 1917 came a constitutional amendment conferring the suffrage, and this amendment was ratified by all but a few of the forty-eight states. Woman suffrage has been a fact since 1920.

It is amusing to look back—and forward—with regard to this important question. The melancholy predictions with regard to the effects of woman suffrage have had very little justification in reality. It was said that the vote would cheapen women, that they were physically unfit for the rough work of the ballot box, that they would be easily swayed by emotion, that they would fall a prey to demagogues. There is little concrete evidence to sustain these generalizations. On the other hand, it must be confessed, some of the more strident advocates of woman suffrage painted a picture a little closer to the millennium than the facts of the years after 1920 suggest. After all, as I find it pleasant to remind my more feminist friends, the first national election in which women voted was one in which they trooped to the polls to cast their ballots for Warren Gamaliel Harding.

But the point does not lie here. Liberalism and woman suffrage are closely identified, because they both rest upon the principle of the maximum respect for the individual personality. Is there, as we see it today, any sound reason to believe that women are any less discriminating than men? Are they to be considered as intellectually or morally inferior to men? Are we to assume that they, less than men, have interests and ideals which they may wish to protect at the polls? Woman suffrage has come in the United States not as a political nostrum, not even as a means of elevating politics, but as a recognition of the equal and dignified relationship which ought to exist between the sexes in a democracy. And this is its fundamental justification.

But let us go back to the late eighteenth and early nineteenth century. One of the great causes connected with liberalism is that of the spread of education. It could hardly be otherwise. Thomas Jefferson, always a pioneer, had drawn up an ambitious program for public education in Virginia before the years of the Revolution. But the great movement for the development of public schools came much later, and is perhaps most conveniently identified with the name of Horace Mann. It would be wrong, no doubt, to draw too sharp a distinction between conservatives and liberals, so far as education is concerned. Yet the fact remains that the opposition to free public education naturally came from the American right. It came from people who simply could not see any use in raising people out of the status in which God had placed them. It came from people who did not see why they should pay taxes for the benefit of somebody else. It came in part from the more fortunate classes of the community. And so in the broad sense of the term, we may connect the great sweep of educational reform with liberalism.

In the period before the Civil War, liberalism was still largely connected with the removing of restrictions on others. I shall not speak here of the antislavery movement but shall reserve treatment of it for another essay. But expedients like the abolition of imprisonment for debt, the repeal of mechanics' lien laws, and the like, illustrate the point. It is perhaps still more important that the struggle against business concentration, typified by the conflict of Andrew Jackson with the Bank of the United States, also took a negative form. Jackson was probably right in viewing with alarm the power of this private institution. But his point of view was highly negative; he had no constructive solution of the banking problem to offer. In this emphasis on preventing something, rather than on using the authority of the state for positive ends, he was typical enough of his time.

But American liberalism wears a different guise after the period of the Civil War. Slowly, and at first with many setbacks, those who called themselves liberals began to realize that it was not enough to set men free from religious restrictions, or economic restrictions, or the harassments of ignorance. The power of the state was to be exercised positively for the improvement of the social order, for the prevention of the abuse of power by the increasingly influential business class. This view needed some time to take root. The great business leaders of the late half of the nineteenth century were by no means kindly disposed to it. John D. Rockefeller, in many ways a not unadmirable figure, seems to have assumed that there was a kind of natural hostility between himself and government. He did not think of obedience to the law as a social duty imposed upon him as the mandate of society. He was playing a game. In 1902, when Theodore Roosevelt started suit against the Northern Securities Association, J. P. Morgan came to him and said in effect, "I'll send my man down to see you and we'll fix it up." Implicit in his remark was the idea of a deal between business and government on equal terms. It was against this conception that liberalism had to contend.

One of the first instances of the limitation of a business group by the national government was the Interstate Commerce Act of 1887, which at least made a start on the regulation of the railroads in the public interest. The trust prosecutions, first initiated with real vigor by Theodore Roosevelt, were an attempt to free the society from excessive domination by small groups of businessmen. The Federal Reserve Act asserted the interest of the public in the operation of the banking system. The Pure Food and Drug Act protected the consumer against noxious or deleterious products. The list of measures of this kind could of course be lengthened.

But the more significant changes came, not in the first two decades of the century, but with the advent of the New Deal. In the first place, the principle of public regulation was extended. The stock market was brought under public control. The great utilities, which had so egregiously abused their power in the twenties, were subjected to regulation. The banking system was placed beyond the domination of private bankers, and a public agency, the Federal Reserve Board, was given increased authority. But there were great changes in other ways. The policies of the twenties were especially regardful of the position of the businessman. No rational man denies that these interests deserved to be considered, but in the thirties the federal government turned to give a new consideration to the worker and the agriculturist. The measures enacted in this period were by no means perfect, and they ought not to be so regarded. But what they were intended to do was in line with the essence of American liberalism, that is, to set up countervailing power to the power of American capitalism. The principle was sound. Finally, in the true spirit of liberalism, measures more sweeping than ever before were taken for the relief of the unfortunate and the unemployed. At the same time, a great program of social security was initiated, which could have no other object than to prevent the suffering that comes from unemployment and from the misfortune and dependency that often accompanies old age. Finally, the unfortunate and the distressed were assisted in the most sweeping program of relief ever attempted by the federal government. This program involved deficit financing, and it ran counter to the views of many staunch conservatives. Yet it certainly did not wreck the country, and it may have prevented very grave social unrest. At any rate, it was a new expression of the spirit of American liberalism.

The interesting thing about the measures we have outlined is that they have stood the test of time. There have been modifications, yes, as, for example, when the Taft-Hartley Law supplanted the Wagner Act. But who proposes to abandon regulation of the stock market and of the issuance of securities? Who is there today that would think that the great power interests of the country ought not to be controlled at all? Who is there that does not approve of the present status of the Federal Reserve Board? Who thinks we ought to break up the labor unions? Who is there that would not recognize some kind of responsibility on the part of government for the spread between agricultural and industrial prices? Who is there that would not recognize a paramount duty on the part of government to take far-reaching measures to deal with a future depression? The answer to these rhetorical questions is not an unqualified "no one." Dissentients still exist. But there is little difference between the two political parties in these matters, and there is little reason to suppose that the clock will be turned back. Indeed, it is a common observation that the Eisenhower administration not only proceeded in many ways along the line of the New Deal, but reconciled many persons to what was done over two decades ago.

What does liberalism mean in the field of international affairs? The optimism which is a constituent part of liberalism is seen in foreign policy in anti-imperialism and nonintervention. Those who described themselves as liberals were in general very skeptical of the desirability of imposing American rule on others. This is not to say that all of them were doctrinaires in this regard. But in general they believed that the United States, when it acquired control of territory or peoples which could not be directly assimilated into the Union, should be responsible for preparing them for independence and granting them such independence in due course. Frequently they had what may have been an exaggerated faith in the possibility of transplanting democratic institutions. But this was the direction in which they wished to move. In the same way, it was liberal opinion which sustained the good neighbor policy, which finally led to the withdrawal of the American marines from Haiti and the Dominican Republic and Nicaragua, which abrogated the treaties with Panama and Cuba by which we had reserved to ourselves the right of intervention in the affairs of these states, which brought about those two great declarations at Montevideo and Buenos Aires by which the United States solemnly pledged itself not to interfere in the external or internal affairs of the other American republics. It was liberal opinion which looked to the idea of a closer collaboration of the states of this hemisphere and placed itself behind the movement known as Pan-Americanism. I am not saying that this point of view was confined to liberals. But it is closely associated with the names of Woodrow Wilson and Franklin Roosevelt, two great liberal presidents.

Liberalism takes an enlarged rather than a narrow view of what constitutes the national interest in the field of foreign affairs. Characteristic of American liberalism is the movement for closer collaboration in the interests of peace. And here we come again to the great name of Woodrow Wilson. His vision of a world which should be united against war was in the liberal tradition. In the great struggle over the League of Nations in 1919 and 1920, conservatives, though in many cases freely admitting the desirability of machinery for the adjustment of international disputes, were loth to bind the United States to common action with other states for the preservation of peace. It may be said that the idea of collective security, which Wilson sought to promote, was an iridescent dream. In the broad sense it may be. But in the campaign tour of 1919 Wilson stressed the idea again and again that if the world did not concert measures against war, the children that gathered around his car would be the victims of a new war. His words were not heeded, either in the United States or in Europe. There was much truth in them, as the melancholy events of 1939–1945 were clearly to show. And even if we reject today as impracticable the idea of collective security, we have come to see that the peace of the world can be preserved only if the United States is ready to act with other nations to maintain it. The alliances by which the United States is bound today are the practical expression of this point of view.

The staunch conservative would look with some skepticism upon the use of American economic power to promote a more stable economic order abroad. Yet, in 1947 and the years that followed, we made the great experiment that is known as the Marshall Plan. We were no doubt acting from an enlarged view of the national interest. We ought not to be too smug about what we did. Yet there was generosity as well as calculation in the policy we followed, and it is not without reason that Winston Churchill described the Marshall Plan as the "most unsordid act in history." It took imagination and daring to carry out that policy; it took faith rather than doubt in the possibilities of the future. Much the same thing can be said with regard to the Point Four program, aborted as our efforts in this regard have often been. Our agreement to supply India with foodstuffs on generous terms was justifiable only if we believe that by acts of this kind we may not only serve our own interest but also be helpful to others.

Liberalism is the enemy of a narrow and restricted nationalism. It sees the importance of freer trade relationships, as opposed to a dogmatic protectionism. It hopes for agreement and understanding, looking at some time in the future to the effective limitation of armaments and to the use of the new energies that man has released for peaceful purposes. It is implicit in President Eisenhower's open-sky proposal, in the Baruch-Acheson plan for the control of atomic armaments put forward a decade ago, in plans for an international agreement on the pacific use of atomic energy. Of course the line here is not entirely clear. Many conservatives, conservatives in domestic politics, have been wise enough to see the desirability of measures such as these. But the hopeful view of what is to come that these plans embody, the conviction that man can shape the future in ways that will benefit not only a single nation, but wide areas of the world, is more characteristic of the liberal temper than the skepticism which insists that the problems are virtually insoluble.

Closely connected with all these matters is the temper that seeks to understand the conduct and the interests of others, that is tolerant of dissent and generous in judgment as well as in action. The blatant appeal to fear and suspicion, the agitation of the demagogue who plays upon these age-old weaknesses of the human species, the technique which operates on the assumption that suppression is the answer to unpleasant or heterodox ideas and which identifies all search for a better world with the philosophy of our enemies, the exaggerated fear which strikes at the liberty of the individual in the name of national security and which judges intellectual error and confusion as the equivalent of treason, all these things are repudiated by the American liberal. And the reaction against Senator McCarthy which in time drove the senator from the front page of our newspapers, and relegated him to something very like obscurity, was the affirmation of the liberal tradition. It is in the same spirit that Telford Taylor wrote his great book on civil rights; it is in the same spirit that that grand old man of the bar, John Lord O'Brian, delivered the Godkin Lectures at Harvard in 1955. Respect for the integrity of the human personality is of the essence of liberalism.

It is not to be supposed that the liberal cannot go wrong. His optimism, his sympathy with human suffering and weakness, his sometimes impatient desire for the attainment of an ideal goal may lead him into error and prevent him from seeing the impracticability or the possibly unhappy consequences of what look to him like measures of improvement. There will be for him, no doubt, moments of disillusion. But at bottom he will retain his faith.

And the key word is faith. Man is indeed, from one angle of vision, a miserable being, tormented by fear, racked by unnecessary passion, the victim of his own follies and his own delusions. But if man has fear, he has also hope. And if he has hate, he has also love. If he can err most grievously and can destroy, he can also build. The liberal tradition in America is the record of his aspirations and his faith, and when, if ever, these things pass, America, as we know and honor it, will have passed too.

Radicalism in America

THE prevailing political tendencies in the United States, we have insisted in a preceding essay, have been almost always those of moderation. But occasionally the opposite has been true, and it is therefore necessary to examine the history of American radicalism. We shall, however, go far astray in any such inquiry if we are not particularly careful at the outset to define precisely what it is that we are talking about. The word "radical" is a smear word in America, and, until we take the smear out of it and examine the real inner meaning of the term, we shall not be able to approach any useful analysis.

Radicalism, for the purposes of this essay, is to be defined as the advocacy or accomplishment of drastic social, political, or economic change. The emphasis is on the word "drastic," for very obviously no society is completely static, and the most healthy ones are constantly engaged in a process of adjustment. From this point of view, most of the major great developments in American political life cannot justly be described as radical.

Take, for example, the American Revolution. Viewed from the angle of domestic or internal history, the Revolution can hardly be described as a radical movement at all. As Dr. John Franklin Jameson long ago showed in his interesting volume *The American Revolution Considered as a Social Movement*, the changes that were made in the internal order were, on the whole, very moderate ones. There was some extension of the suffrage; there was some change in the land system—not enough, by any means, to alter the fundamental nature of the economy—there was some alteration of emphasis in the political structure of the states. But none of these things was a "drastic" modification of what existed; none of them represented a distinct breach with the past. The American society of 1775 was not revolutionized by 1787; on the contrary, the conservative interests of the country were in the ascendancy by the latter date.

The charge of radicalism was brought at the time against William Jennings Bryan in the campaign of 1896. I have already stated in an earlier essay that it seems to me fortunate that the American people turned their backs on the boy orator of the Platte in the election of that year. But it does not follow that the free-silver movement was truly radical. In the perspective of today, with so many experiments in currency manipulation all over the world to remember, with our own devaluation, with the frequent devaluations in other lands, we can see clearly that the social, economic, and political order is not necessarily shaken to its depths by tinkering with the currency. We do not have to believe that such tinkering is a sovereign specific for social or economic evils to recognize this essential fact.

It is the same way with the New Deal. It is high time that the New Deal be judged without passion, since what it wrought in the way of change is three decades behind us. In the light of today, we can see that the innovations of the thirties involved no fundamental change in the American economic order and that in its broad lines the American system of private enterprise and private opportunity was by no means shaken by the reforms of that period. Indeed, it can be contended (as it *has* been contended), and with some cogency, that essentially the purposes of the Roosevelt administration and the policies of the Roosevelt administration were aimed at insulating the American system against the danger of revolution or violence, rather than at accomplishing a revolution. This is a matter we cannot here examine, but no one who observes the current order of things, the large role of the business classes, and the attention paid to their viewpoint is likely to maintain that there has been a drastic change in the American way of life. The balance of power between economic groups has most certainly shifted; but the essentials of the economic order have not been subverted.

There have been, however, as I see it, a few major radical movements in American history. These movements are the abolition of slavery and the immediate enfranchisement of the Negro which followed on it, the prohibition movement, and the anarchist and communist movements. Only the first two of these movements, antislavery

and prohibition, ever attracted a following so substantial
as to have a fundamental effect upon the actual political
conduct of the American people; only one of them succeeded in the long run; and this one succeeded only in
lifting the chains of slavery, and not in the full recognition of the rights of the Negro as a citizen.

Before examining these specific movements, it may be
worth while to meditate for a little as to the nature of the
radical mind and as to the place of the radical in the
scheme of things, not with a view to discovering anything
particularly novel but with the purpose of understanding
a little better what it is that makes men act in such
a context. At the root of most radicalism lies a passionate
belief in Utopia. The radical is a man whose sense of
difficulties is blunted—one might almost say destroyed—
by his sense of injustice, whose vision of the future dis-
torts his insight into the problems of the present. He is, in
the nature of the case, intolerant, convinced of his own
righteousness and, almost equally certainly, of the un-
righteousness of others. In the nature of the case, he will
be quite indifferent to vested interest. More moderate
men may reflect that those who benefit most (and perhaps unduly) from a given social order are themselves
not the responsible creators of that order and that, when
changes are to be made, those persons who through no
fault of their own possess this or that special privilege and
enjoy an economic status which, in a large view, appears
inequitable yet have some claim to consideration. The
radical will take little account of such ideas. The confis-
cation of a property interest will not appear to him as a

wrong done to an individual but as a necessary incident of the social transformation which he proposes to effect. And he may well go further and decide that nothing, not even the individual life, should stand in the way of his goal. He may view with sympathy the use of physical force to bring about his new society. He cannot be too choosy about method if the end in view is to be attained. While his objective may be a generous one, even a noble one, he himself may not be generous. The hate which he feels toward those who stand in his way is often fully as powerful as the love he bears to those whom he hopes to rescue from oppression.

The question may be raised as to whether society would be better off without him. Would it not be much more comfortable if the extremist elements of society did not exist at all? Is not the presence of the radical one of those unfortunate things that all reasonable people should deprecate? One can hardly believe so. It is the function of the radical to awaken us from complacency, to goad us into action, not for the attainment of his own goals but for the improvement of the social order. The penalty fixed for a static society which pays insufficient attention to its own inequalities, which is deaf to the grievances of the discontented and the maltreated, is often a very heavy one indeed; it may, in fact, be nothing less than revolution. A few strident voices which arouse the average man from complacency, which shock him into sensibility, which provoke in the more intelligent and better balanced conservative or liberal a disposition at least to consider some remedy for the conditions complained of, are useful in any society. Every social and economic order is more healthy, more likely to deal efficiently with its own complex problems if it is subject to criticism. "Challenge and response," to use Arnold Toynbee's phrase, is the law of life. The extremist may be entirely wrong in his prescription, and in many cases he can be shown to be wrong; but his diagnosis is not completely to be cast aside.

We can look at the matter from a little different point of view. Whether we like it or not, there will be in every society some who disapprove of it, burn with indignation at its injustices and abuses, and have an easy and pat remedy to correct them. What we ought to be doing is to count these people, to take warning from an increase in their numbers, and to prepare and execute a program which draws the fangs of their discontents. Mere suppression is no adequate answer to the men of the extreme left. And, as a matter of fact, we have a very striking example of this in our own history.

For, in the great crusade against slavery, just such suppression was attempted. In his annual message of 1835, Andrew Jackson (sometimes the rather extravagantly admired hero of the "liberals") recommended to the Congress the passage of legislation excluding abolition literature from the mails. His recommendation was not acted upon; but in 1836 the House of Representatives passed by a vote of 117 to 68 a resolution declaring that "all petitions, memorials, resolutions, propositions or papers relating in any way or to any extent whatever to the subject of slavery or the abolition of slavery shall, without being either printed or referred, be laid upon the table and that no further action whatever shall be had thereon." It was this resolution which initiated one of the most amazing parliamentary struggles in our history. At the time the resolution was passed, John Quincy Adams, former president of the United States and then a member of Congress, denounced it as "a direct violation of the Constitution of the United States, of the rules of this House, and of the rights of my constituents." Up to this time Adams, though deeply convinced of the evil of slavery, had played no conspicuous part in attacking it. But now that the issue was transformed into one of freedom of petition, he became aroused. For years he struggled against the "gag rule," as it was quite properly called, and in his contest against it he discussed again and again the general question of slavery. The ill-judged action of the men of the South and their allies, far from allaying the slavery controversy, had, in practice, made it more bitter. The public debate went on; the gag rule itself was repealed in 1844; the discussion of the problem became wider and wider and more and more envenomed. Those who imagine that they can exorcise a radical point of view by plain suppression ought to reflect upon this historic controversy of more than a century ago. The violation of constitutional rights is no legitimate answer to any form of agitation.

Let us examine further the question of abolition and see what we can learn from some analysis of its past. It is first to be noted that the abolitionists, in the literal and correct use of the word, were always a very small fraction of the total population. It is not easy to say how many persons actually joined the various abolitionist societies in the various states, but the number was probably never more than fifty thousand. The two national parties, the Whig and Democratic parties, never committed themselves to abolition, and the Republican party was pledged until 1864, not to the elimination of slavery but to opposition to the further extension of slavery. The only national party that ever took a more forthright stand on the issue was the Liberty party, which presented a candidate for the presidency in 1840 and in 1844. In the first of these two elections it polled something over seven thousand votes. In the election of 1844 it polled about twenty thousand votes, holding the balance of power in the state of New York and contributing in some measure to the defeat of Henry Clay in the election for the presidency. But from 1844 onward, though undoubtedly the country was becoming more and more aroused to the evil of slavery, the antislavery sentiment of the North found its chief expression, not in seeking the extinction of the "peculiar institution," but in confining it within its existing boundaries. The American people showed on this, as on most questions, that attitude of political moderation that has usually characterized them. They were "liberals," not radicals.

The abolition movement was not only weak numerically but it was ridden with faction. William Lloyd Garrison, who has sometimes quite incorrectly been regarded as the very head and front of the agitation, was unable to co-operate with others, and the Massachusetts society was in constant hot water with the societies of the Middle West. The American Anti-Slavery Society was rent with feuds of the bitterest description, and it was virtually dissolved in 1840. It had never been affluent, and it was financially disorganized at the time of the schism.

Yet it cannot be denied that the cause to which the abolitionists dedicated themselves succeeded as it deserved to succeed. Why was this so? One fundamental reason was that the sentiment against human slavery was widespread in the Western world in the first half of the nineteenth century. It is an error to imagine that the United States in any sense led the way in dealing with this immense evil. The French Revolution had abolished slavery in Haiti as early as 1793; by 1860 slavery had disappeared in almost every one of the Latin-American states; the British abolished slavery in the British West Indies by a system of gradual emancipation in 1833; the Second French Republic wiped out the evil in 1848. Only Spain and Brazil, in the Western world, retained the slave system at the time when matters came to a head in the United States. Against a tide of opinion so sweeping as this it was impossible to remain inert and indifferent.

In the second place, it is to be observed that the evil of the system was a sectional evil. In a sense this made it more difficult to deal with, since it rent the Union in twain and put in hazard the precious fabric which had been woven in 1787. But, in another sense, the fact that the slave power was confined to only a part of the country made it easier to rally opinion against it. It was not hard for northern men and women to become indignant about a social system which did not directly jeopardize their own interests or call upon them for any sacrifice.

In the third place, and most important of all, the abolition of slavery was very much in line with the American tradition and the American temper. It is a most striking historical fact that the only radical movement which thoroughly succeeded in the United States was *libertarian*. It involved no extension of the power of government over the individual; it was not only thoroughly consistent with, but virtually an extension of, the doctrine of free enterprise; it was based on the great American dogma that every man had a right to an opportunity to rise in the world; it involved not the repudiation but the reaffirmation of the historic principles on which America was founded. Its success does not suggest that the radicalisms of our own day, involving the exaggeration and perversion of the power of the state, will in any way appeal to the American people or that the radical doctrines of the twentieth century will find a secure lodgment in the United States.

Indeed, the *manner* in which the abolition movement succeeded offers a good deal of evidence of the moderation of the American people. The extreme opponents of American slavery, as we have said, were never a very large section of the population; and as late as 1861 the country might have been well content with a solution of the problem which would have forbidden the further extension of the evil and would have looked to its "ultimate extinction," in Lincoln's phrase, through the slow passage of time. It is a fact not to be forgotten that as late as 1861, and in the Lincoln administration, Congress was ready to assure the South that it intended no assault upon its domestic institutions. Even after the possibility of compromise was barred by the secession of the South, action was slow. The Emancipation Proclamation was a gesture, a highly important gesture, but still a gesture rather than a measure of far-reaching import in the practical sense; it freed the slaves behind the southern lines. The Thirteenth Amendment was not even adopted by the Congress until after the elections of 1864; to put the matter another way, it needed the successful outcome of a civil war to bring an end to slavery in the United States. In view of all these considerations and the facts we have already cited with regard to the disappearance of slavery in other parts of the Western world, it can hardly be stated that, in dealing with this terrible evil, the American people were rash, impulsive, or innately revolutionary. On the contrary, they showed themselves deeply reluctant to challenge the past or to overturn the vested interests that had established themselves in the South. It is important to bear these facts in mind, and they shed some light, also, on the second of the movements that I intend to discuss in this essay, the enfranchisement of the Negro in the South.

As we approach this question, there may be some of my readers who will question the use of the word "radical" in connection with the extension of the suffrage to the Negro in the reconstruction years. The suffrage, it may be maintained, is an inherent right of the citizen.

The Negro needs it, and has always needed it for the protection of his rights and interests. This point of view deserves respect and, as I have said, in contemporary conditions, acceptance. But the immediate enfranchisement of a mass of freemen, by far the larger part of whom were totally illiterate and utterly untrained in the art of self-government (and self-government *is* an art), may, without an undue extension of language, be described as a drastic political change and therefore falling within the definition of "radical" which I gave at the beginning of this essay. We shall consider it here without denying that, as a matter of abstract justice and in the context of today, our colored population ought to have a full and equal participation in the rights and privileges which belong to every American citizen.

The time has long since gone by to consider the period of reconstruction in the South as a kind of saturnalia of ignorance, corruption, and folly. We know today that much of the region made substantial educational progress, that the measures taken by the state legislatures did not prevent a remarkable economic recovery on the comparative basis with the ante-bellum period, that the peculations and extravagances of southern state legislatures were matched and indeed exceeded by northern politicians. We may—and should—condemn the measures taken in the last decade of the century to restrict or nullify the Negro vote and consolidate the rule of the white man. Yet it is an objective fact that Negro suffrage in the South did not survive and that in many southern states various expedients were succesfully adopted to keep the black man from the polls. We cannot therefore say that this reform succeeded. When it came to the question of attempting to *enforce* Negro suffrage, the North drew back. The famous Force bill introduced by Senator Henry Cabot Lodge in 1890, which would have put the power of the federal government behind the Fifteenth Amendment, passed the House but died in committee in the Senate. The rest of the country was not disposed to force the issue to an ultimate conclusion. It valued the unity of the sections more than it did the principle of nondiscrimination at the polls. The question remains whether it is possible by legal enactment or court decision successfully to impose on one part of the nation a social or political reform to which there is widespread local opposition.

With regard to the third of the radical measures which we have enumerated at the beginning of this essay, we can speak with confidence. National prohibition undeniably involved a drastic interference with the habits and predilections of a very large part of our population. It met with substantial opposition and was never effectively enforced. It had to be repealed in 1933. What is the story of this experiment? How did it ever come to be put into effect? What produced the reaction against it and led to its repeal?

The first of these questions is a complicated one and well deserves analysis. In the first place, the misuse of liquor is an undeniable social evil. The extent of this evil may be variously estimated, but no one will deny that it exists. And the movement for temperance, or for total

[69]

abstinence and indeed for prohibition, had a very considerable vogue in the United States long before the Eighteenth Amendment became the law of the land. Among certain of the Protestant sects, notably the Baptists and the Methodists, the prejudice against the use of alcohol was strong. In the South, rigid restrictions on the use of alcohol were often defended on the ground that this was the way to keep liquor away from the Negro. In the North, a certain type of employer saw in similar limitations a means of increasing the efficiency of his labor force. And the strength of the argument for dealing roughly with the liquor traffic was often augmented by the connection between the liquor dealers and corrupt politics and by the blind obscurantism of many of the manufacturers and sellers of alcohol in regard to their own businesses.

These factors, nevertheless, are by no means enough in themselves to explain the triumph of national prohibition. Considered as a separate issue, able to attract the attention of the voters in a new party organization, the movement never amounted to much. The Prohibition party appeared on the ballot in every election from 1876 to 1928. But its maximum vote was never 300,000, and it never, with one possible exception, was successful in influencing a presidential election. Its activity does not explain the adoption of the Eighteenth Amendment.

Probably the greatest single factor in the victory of the "drys" was the efficiency, the hard-boiled efficiency, of the foremost agency for the elimination of the traffic, the Anti-Saloon League. The leaders of the League early discovered the most effective tactic to make their views felt, that is, the tactic of the balance of power. By supporting any candidate who would vote "dry" and by opposing any candidate who was "wet," whatever his personal habits might be, they were able to accomplish great results in the elections to Congress, to terrorize many representatives, and to wield an influence wholly disproportionate to their own numbers.

But they might not have succeeded even then if it had not been for a variety of circumstances, one of which is the method of amending the Constitution of the United States. That method involves a two-thirds vote in both houses of Congress and ratification either by state legislatures or state conventions in three-fourths of the states. Under such conditions, it was always possible to argue that Congress, in sending an amendment to the states for ratification, was doing no more than offering to the people of these states a chance to express themselves on an important question. Conversely, it was possible to argue that a reform which had secured a two-thirds vote in the House of Representatives and in the Senate was one that had great popular support and that the state legislatures ought not to stand in the way of it.

But there was more to the matter than that. Prohibition was, in one of its aspects, a controversy between the urban and the rural way of life. It had its principal support on the farms. Now it so happens that many of the state legislatures in the United States are egregiously gerrymandered in favor of the country districts, while the cities are underrepresented. It was easy, therefore, once the amendment had been submitted, to secure favorable action in ratifying it. Only a few of the most densely populated states held out against the movement.

There is a final factor which perhaps ought to be added to the account. In the second decade of the twentieth century the general climate of opinion in the United States was favorable to reform. The temper of the time was optimistic. If liquor was a social evil, why not wipe it out as expeditiously and completely as possible? In particular, why not do this at a time when the country was engaged in war and when it needed its full energies and resources (including its grain) for the winning of the conflict? It is not mere chance that the Eighteenth Amendment was submitted during the conflict and ratified in 1919.

These various considerations help to explain the extraordinary power behind national prohibition. Yet few measures have been so obviously a failure. After all, a reform that did not reform, and that had to be repealed, will not rank high among the measures of American statesmanship. To repeat what has already been said, the amendment brought with it widespread corruption; it is by no means certain that it decreased the actual consumption of alcohol; it engendered an atmosphere of lawlessness and defiance that was contrary to the interests of the whole community. It put a premium on hypocrisy in politicians, and it distracted the country from other political issues. And within a decade of its enactment, the tide was already running strongly toward repeal.

I turn now to the most interesting radicalisms of all,

those which look to the entire reconstitution of society. There are two extremes of these, anarchism, on the one hand, and communism, on the other. The two may converge, and sometimes have converged. There is no reason, of course, why anarchy, that is, the absence of government, cannot be combined with a voluntary communism, that is, with a sharing of goods. On the other hand, there is nothing inevitable about this conjunction, and the two movements should not be confused.

Anarchism in the United States has been of two kinds. There is, first, philosophical anarchism, which, in stressing the abolition of government, makes no appeal to violence. One of the earliest names is that of Josiah Warren, who founded an anarchist community at Modern Times, Long Island, in the early 1850's. There is a strong anarchist flavor in Thoreau's essay on "Civil Disobedience." William Lloyd Garrison was, at one time in his career, a disbeliever in the right of the state to dictate conduct. A systematic formulation of anarchist beliefs, with much indebtedness to the French anarchist Pierre Joseph Proudhon, is found in the work of Benjamin Tucker, whose journal, *Liberty*, was first published in 1881. Still another name worth mentioning is that of Stephen Pearl Andrews, whose "Science of Society," published at about the same time, developed an ingenious picture of an anarchist society with a sliding-scale system of rewards for labor, depending on the intensity of the application required, the time element, and the degree of skill. But it goes without saying that the native American anarchists had few followers and that their views play a very trivial part in the development of the United States.

There was, however, an indigenous "action" movement in the United States which was closely connected with anarchism and which deserves especial attention. This was the organization known as the Industrial Workers of the World, or Wobblies. In its origins the I.W.W. was extremely diverse, drawing support from the Western Federation of Miners, from a few other unions, from migratory farm workers in the Middle and Far West, and from radical Socialists and Communists. But between 1905 and 1908, after bitter factional fighting, the W.F.M. withdrew, the doctrinaire Communists were driven out, and most of the Socialists lost interest. What was left was a movement which can best be described as anarcho-syndicalism. The basis of this movement was industrial unionism, the ideal, "one big union." The technique was that of violence, rather than political action, of which the I.W.W. was contemptuous. But the final goal was a society in which the workers would control the instruments of production and in which government, in the traditional sense, would be unnecessary. It is highly significant that the most drastic native American movement for the total reformation of the social order not only did not emphasize the all-powerful state but, in its theory at any rate, reacted strongly against authority.

The I.W.W. had a stormy existence. It engineered a series of strikes, of which the most dramatic was that in the textile mills in Lawrence, Massachusetts, in 1912. It carried on a large number of free-speech fights, the most sensational in Centralia, Washington, in 1919. It actively advocated sabotage, and it violently opposed American entrance into World War I. It declined in strength after 1919, partly because of the active efforts of government against its members, and it suffered a new factional split in 1924. After the latter year it was of very minor significance.

Besides the indigenous anarchism of the I.W.W., there was also a foreign brand in the United States which goes back as far as the late 1870's and early 1880's. In the year 1882 the most conspicuous leader of this movement, the German Johann Most, arrived in the United States and re-established here his paper, *Die Freiheit*, which he had previously published abroad. In 1883 a Congress at Pittsburgh (a small affair) drew up an address to the workingmen of America which was a direct incitement to violence. And in 1886 there occurred, as an outgrowth of the foreign anarchist movement, the famous Haymarket riot and one of the most sensational trials in the history of the country. At a meeting of protest against police violence in connection with a strike, a bomb was thrown, and several policemen were either killed or wounded. Arrests followed, and four members of the anarchist group in Chicago were sentenced to death, and three others to imprisonment for varying terms. It is much to be doubted (certainly it was never proven) that the condemned men had had any part in the manufacture or throwing of the bomb, and the trial was conducted with gross violations of the rights of the accused. Popular hysteria triumphed over cool judgment. Nor was this the end of the Haymarket affair. When, in 1893, in one of the most courageous acts in American politics, Governor John P. Altgeld commuted the sentence of three of the men on the ground that there had never been sufficient evidence to convict them, there was a new outburst of public indignation. The episode reflects no credit upon the American democracy.

The Haymarket case is not the only case in which anarchists suffered at the hands of a biased judicial tribunal and of an excited public opinion. In the year 1920 two men, Nicola Sacco and Bartolomeo Vanzetti, were accused of the murder of a paymaster at Brockton, Massachusetts. There was no question of their radicalism, and Sacco, at any rate, had evaded the draft. But no motive for the murder was shown; there was no evidence that they had in their possession any of the funds that were stolen; there was no suggestion in their past lives that they were criminally inclined. The decision of the trial court came under grave criticism after their conviction, and it was widely believed that they had been condemned on insufficient evidence by a jury which was prejudiced against them on account of their opinions and which was not impartially charged by the trial judge. The case was appealed and became a matter of widespread public agitation. No less a person than Felix Frankfurter, later a Supreme Court justice, took up the cause of the condemned men. Though the Massachusetts Supreme Court sustained the verdict, many persons were not satisfied.

The governor then appointed a committee of three distinguished citizens to review the matter, and this committee also justified the conviction. The two men were electrocuted on August 27, 1927. Despite the action of the higher court and the committee, the gravest doubt still subsists today as to whether justice was done. Certainly no one can read the history of the case without taking thought as to the capacity of the average American, in times of stress, to judge fairly those of radical leanings. Certainly, in this as in the Haymarket affair, there is a challenge to all of us to exercise wisdom and discretion and, if necessary, courage in dealing justly with those of whose views we disapprove.

Before we leave the subject of anarchism, a few other facts might be noted. President McKinley met his death at the hands of a foreign anarchist in 1901; the steel magnate Henry Clay Frick was assaulted by an anarchist in 1902; one of the most colorful figures in the history of American radicalism, Emma Goldman, was an anarchist; the anarchist movement played a part in opposition to World War I; and in the mass deportations which followed the war, another example of summary and hardly justifiable legal process, many anarchists were included. But the movement has little importance after 1919, and we may therefore turn to what was far more significant in the years that followed, the development of communism in the United States.

The earliest true examples of communism in the history of the United States are the voluntary communities which sprang up, not in recent times but in the period

before the Civil War and even at a much earlier period—
such communities, for example, as those of the Shakers,
which go back to the latter part of the eighteenth century
or that extraordinary group known as the Oneida Per-
fectionists. The story of these societies, many of them
religious in character, is in many ways a fascinating one.
It is told in detail in the work of John Pierpoint Noyes.
But it is fair to say that these various groups left no real
impression on American life and consequently merit no
detailed consideration. Their story is one of curiosities
rather than of significant manifestations of American
radicalism. What we mean today when we speak of communism is really totalitarian socialism based, not on the
equal sharing of goods but on the control by the state of
all the means of production, and on the operation of the
great industrial machine by a party or personal dictator-
ship. Such a movement has never had any roots whatever
in American life, and it is not likely to have. It has never
commanded a significantly wide support among native
Americans. Yet it has developed, nonetheless, on American soil and is of substantial historical importance.
Where are we to look for its origins, and what are the
fundamental considerations with regard to it?

Marxian socialism, out of which modern socialist to-
talitarianism has grown, came to the United States in the
late 1860's. But it is by no means clear that all of the early
Marxists in America were really revolutionaries; certainly they were not conspirators. One of the great
Marxian dialecticians in the United States, one of the
subtlest minds in the Marxism of the nineteenth century,

was Daniel De Leon, who was born in Curaçao but came early in life to the United States and became the dominant figure in the nineties in the direction of what was known as the Socialist Labor party. De Leon believed in a twin attack upon the evils of capitalism, through political agitation on the one hand and through the development of industrial unionism on the other. The political group in which he played so large a role appeared upon the ballot as early as 1892. It never polled a substantial vote, and the greater part of its support came from immigrant groups in the city of New York. The language of its platforms suggests the seizure of power by the workers and the reconstitution of the state under worker control. But De Leon himself by no means clearly advocated the use of force; in fact, there are passages in his writings which indicate the precise opposite. Nor did the Socialist Labor party exert any significant influence. What Americans thought of communism before World War I may be partly indicated by the fact that the *Encyclopaedia Britannica*, edited in America, in its eleventh edition (1902–1910) does not even mention the Socialist Labor party, or for that matter Karl Marx, in its article on communism.

The Bolshevik revolution of 1917 naturally gave an impetus to the Communist ideology. But whoever reads its history in detail will be impressed by the factionalism characteristic of the early movement, the constant splits and dissension in the Communist ranks, and the limited nature of its appeal. The Communist party appeared under its own name on the ballot in 1928 and again in 1932, but in this latter year, after the gruelling depression of the preceding period, it succeeded in polling only about 100,000 votes in over 38,000,000.

There is little doubt, however, that the depression gave to the party a strength which it had never had before. The significant fact, in the early thirties, is the migration of a substantial group of the intellectuals into its ranks. In the elections of 1932, fifty-two prominent writers and publicists, among them such men as Edmund Wilson, John Dos Passos, and Matthew Josephson formally endorsed the candidacy of William Z. Foster, the Communist standard bearer. In the universities Communist study groups sprang up. In the labor unions Communists became active, and beyond all question some of them penetrated into the government, into the National Labor Board, the Department of Agriculture, the Treasury, and the Department of State. The philosophy behind this development ought to be understood, though not approved. The United States seemed to be far from solving its internal problems; misery and unemployment were widespread; on the other hand, as the propagandists had it, Russia was moving ahead under the five-year plan. In 1936 the Soviet Union formulated a "democratic" constitution, and, though the guarantees contained in it were intended merely to deceive the naïve, they were by some simple souls taken for what they said. The Communists at this time made great play of co-operating with liberal groups anxious to see the amelioration of the social order; these were the days of the Popular Front. Still more, they professed themselves to be the friends of peace and the enemies of fascism and of national socialism. It should not be unintelligible that to the young, the ardent, and the inexperienced they seemed not sinister agents of Moscow but collaborators in the search for a better world.

Practically speaking, the high point of Communist influence was undoubtedly in the thirties. Many of the intellectuals were driven out of the movement when Stalin made his cynical bargain with Hitler in 1939; and still more were disillusioned when the "imperialist" war of 1939 and 1940 became the great struggle for democracy as soon as Russia itself was attacked. The end of the war carried still further the process we have been describing; the conduct of the Russian government brought more and more people to see how sinister its intentions were; the ruthless suppression of democratic institutions in every country where the Russian authority prevailed was widely resented in the United States; and communism became more and more closely identified with enmity to this country, as indeed it should have been. It became clear that the American party was an instrument of Russian espionage, that at least some of its members acted as Russian agents and as such had penetrated into the government itself, and that its object was to embroil the situation at home rather than to contribute to social progress in any specific sense. The reaction was a violent one; the labor unions, with rare exceptions, turned on their Communist members and drove them out of their ranks; the government arrested and tried the most conspicuous members of the Communist apparatus; and the party itself, if we are to accept (as we well may) the word of Mr. Edgar Hoover, has shrunk greatly in size since the days of the thirties. In 1954 it was declared illegal by a legislative act of the Congress of the United States.

The most interesting question with regard to communism in the United States is the question as to how the American people have reacted to it, and with what degree of rationality. What is the record in this regard? If one looks at the whole history, the first thing that strikes the eye is that there have been two periods in which public opinion, or a segment of it, has overdramatized the danger from the new doctrine and, in striking out against the danger, has jeopardized American libertarian ideals and the rights of innocent citizens.

The first of these came in 1919. It is explicable that America should have suffered from a fit of nerves at that time. During the war period itself there had been much intolerance. The radical elements in the United States had opposed the conflict; and they had been often roughly handled in the courts in decisions under the so-called sedition acts, which sometimes went far beyond the bounds of reason. In addition, with the Bolshevik revolution of 1917 there was presented to the American people the spectacle, in Russia, of a revolutionary order which challenged the assumptions of their way of life. There had been substantial unrest in the United States itself; a series of strikes, including a police strike in Boston, a number of bombing outrages, including the bombing of the house of A. Mitchell Palmer, Attorney

General of the United States; May Day parades accompanied by street fighting in Boston and Cleveland; and a clash of obscure origin in Centralia, Washington, which had resulted in the death of four servicemen and the lynching of one other.

But the "red scare" of 1919–1920 was not of long duration; by the middle of 1920 the country had turned to other matters. A clear evidence of the reaction is to be found in the failure of the Congress to enact a peace-time sedition law. Moreover, though there was a period of raids and arrests on a substantial scale, the action of the federal government was directed largely against aliens, some of whom were undoubtedly apostles of violence in the precise sense of the word. This is not to say that there were no excesses. The deportations which took place were not only carried on without any opportunity for the deportees to be heard, but also they certainly bore no definite relationship to concrete acts forbidden by law. And in the states of the union at the same time there was a rash of statutes directed against criminal anarchy, which were in some cases applied against American citizens whose offense lay in their opinions, not in their deeds.

But the public reaction against the radical in the early period bears little resemblance to what happened in the fifties. Again the historian will not find it difficult to understand the origins of the strongly emotional anti-communism of recent years. The conduct of the government in the Kremlin, its shameless disregard of freedom, was bound to produce a powerful reaction. The striking case of espionage represented by the Fuchs case in Canada, the conviction of Alger Hiss in this country, the revelations of Whittaker Chambers, all combined to arouse apprehension. And, in addition, a skillful demagogue arose to exploit this sentiment and, by adroit publicity, to agitate still further the public mind. In circumstances such as these it is understandable that we went much further in taking measures against the radical than we did in 1919.

The principal evidences of this concern are found in the development of an elaborate administrative mechanism to investigate the loyalty of government employees and in legislation to deal with subversion, notably the so-called McCarran Act of 1950, and the act outlawing the Communist party passed in 1954.

It is not feasible in this brief essay to discuss this matter in detail. It has been brilliantly examined in such books as Zechariah Chafee, Jr.'s, *The Blessings of Liberty*, in Telford Taylor's *Grand Inquest*, and in the Godkin Lectures of John Lord O'Brian under the title *National Security and Individual Freedom*.

In attempting to deal with a problem which everyone admits exists, we at times applied the principle of guilt by association and, without reference to overt acts, gave administrative officials power to decide questions of loyalty without adequate protection to the individual. We relied upon secret information supplied by anonymous accusers, and permitted congressional committees to range far and wide in their search for suspects and to impugn the motives of individuals against whom no charge of any kind existed. These measures represented a departure from the traditional standards of American justice and of American law. They would not be justifiable in any circumstances; but, wholly apart from this, the public apprehension which prompted them seems quite out of proportion to the real danger. The Communist party in the United States, as we have already seen, has never been strong and has for some time been growing weaker. It would be difficult to demonstrate that either American domestic or foreign policy was seriously influenced by Communists; the loyalty investigations showed that the number of persons under Communist influence in the government has always been almost minute; and the notion that our decisions on the highest level were in any substantial degree due to Communist influence is pure illusion. As for espionage, the facts of the matter are that a large part of the information purveyed to the Russian government, or to any other government, is drawn from government documents and the discreet and indiscreet published comment of our public men; that, as regards scientific secrets, experience indicates that they cannot in any event be long kept in the exclusive possession of one nation; and that the overwhelming majority of American public servants will have—and have had—nothing to do with spying. To say this is not to say that no precautionary measures need ever to be taken to protect the privacy of diplomatic interchange or to prevent the penetration of military secrets; it is merely to suggest that, under the influence of a strongly felt public mood, the government, in seeking to protect itself, has by no means struck the best possible balance between security and the rights of the individual.

It is, however, hardly right to say that the American attitude toward radicalism has undergone a definite and possibly permanent change for the worse. In the courts, in particular, the reaction against arbitrary measures seems to be gathering strength. The release of tension in international affairs, to the degree that it exists and gains in force, will accelerate this movement. Those who desire some relaxation should reflect upon the place of radicalism in American history in a broad perspective. They should remind themselves of how rarely radical movements have been successful, and how little reason there is for apprehension and extreme measures in combating them in the light of the American past; they should not forget that *no* radical movement (except abolition), as we have defined such movements, has ever been successful for more than a brief time; they should draw comfort from the fact that, in the one case where there *was* success, libertarian and not totalitarian ideas were what triumphed; and, finally, they should assimilate and propagate the greatest lesson of all that our brief analysis of radicalism suggests, that is, that radical movements are the result of abuses which are not checked in time to satisfy the aspirations of many who are not radical. So long as the American people retain the habit of orderly progress, so long as they are alive to the evils of their social and economic order and grapple with them before these ends have become endemic (as did slavery), they need not fear the rolling thunder on the left.

But what of radicalism in international affairs? What of the Communist menace in the world at large? The question is too broad a one for us to treat in this brief essay, though no one will deny its importance. But surely the answer to it depends in part on the picture which the United States presents to the world in the conduct of its domestic affairs. If we deal with our internal problems wisely, if we expand our own economy and provide for a higher and higher standard of living at home, if we maintain free institutions in undiminished vigor, we may be sure that the impact on the rest of the world will be very great indeed. And, if we couple this improvement with wise measures of defense, and with judicious assistance to other states whose orientation is like our own and in which freedom is valued at its true worth, we need not fear the future. There are already signs of inner tension in the Communist states of Europe. If we are loyal to our own ideals, we have a right to believe that those ideals will profoundly influence the conduct and development of other nations which cherish democracy and which wish to move with us into the future.

Socialism in America

IN THE preceding essay, dealing with American radicalism, nothing has been said about American socialism, except as it is also described by the word "communism." This omission is subject to valid criticism, for socialism, at least in theory and under a strict definition, certainly involves drastic changes in the economic order, that is, the transfer to the state of the instruments of production and the state operation of the same. Moreover, even a casual reader of socialist literature would frequently find in the party tracts references to the "revolution" of the future, to the "overturn" of the existing order, and some socialists have been a little careless in their allusions to the possibility of violence.

Nonetheless, if we examine the socialist movement in terms of the socialist parties here and abroad, we will not be much exercised about the drastic transformation of economic life. The appeals to force on the part of one or another excited leader have been little more than verbiage. The actual development of socialist parties has been marked by a willingness to appeal to the ballot box, by the introduction into socialist platforms of all kinds of melioristic measures, and by a kind of gradualism that is far removed from the impatience of the radical. There is, then, some justification for considering socialism in the United States in a different context from that of the radical movements that have been considered in the preceding essay. And its role in American politics is so interesting and suggestive as readily to lend itself to the special treatment that I intend to give it.

The earliest political manifestations of the socialist idea in the United States are to be found in the far from terrifying or inspiring history of the Socialist Labor party. This party, under this name, first appeared in Chicago in 1877. By the end of 1879 it claimed a membership of ten thousand and chapters in twenty-five states. It was for a decade or more a feeble affair, often wracked by divided counsels, but it picked up a little under the leadership of Daniel De Leon in the nineties. De Leon was a theoretician and dialectician of considerable distinction. He can hardly be described as a great party leader. Vain, domineering, jealous of others, he was, to use Daniel Bell's vivid phrase, "a mechanical giant in a doll's house." The Socialist Labor party nominated a candidate for president in 1892 and polled 21,000 votes; it polled 36,000 in 1896, but it never became an important influence on the American political scene. The three things to remember are that it was Marxist in origin, that it contained chiefly foreign-born, and that its chieftain was not a believer in violence as the road to the new order.

The Socialist party was something else again. It was, to

a greater degree than is always realized, indigenous; it contained many elements besides the Marxists; and, although it was never near a great electoral triumph, it has a history which is infinitely more significant than that of its rival. In order to understand this history, it is necessary to go back into the nineties and take account of the various movements of opinion that combined to produce this new apparition on the American scene.

One of these movements was what was known as Nationalism, and it arose just at the turn of the decade of the nineties. It owed its origin to a book famous at the time entitled *Looking Backward*, written by Edward Bellamy, the son of a Congregational clergyman. At the time that he wrote, Bellamy had not read a word about Marx. He was impressed, as were many others, with the abuses incident to the American social order, with the tendency toward larger and larger business units, and with the growing influence of these units in the affairs of government. In his fanciful novel he tells the story of a man who, after a long sleep, woke up in the year 2000 to discover that society had undergone radical changes, that the instruments of production were now in the control of the state, that the work of production was carried on by an industrial army directed by the state, that the products of industry were shared by all the members of the society, and that peace and plenty reigned. The story bears all the marks of the Victorian age, particularly in the minor role, largely decorative, which was assigned to women. It made a tremendous sensation when it first appeared; it sold over half a million copies; Nationalist clubs were organized in many different parts of the United States; and it seemed for a little while as if a substantial movement might arise. In a few years the whole thing petered out; but it left an impress, nonetheless, and the popularity of *Looking Backward* was an interesting sign of the times.

Contemporaneous with the Nationalist movement is that known as Christian Socialism. The teaching of the social gospel in the churches, so interestingly described by Professor Henry May, was not necessarily connected with the acceptance of the socialist creed. But many ministers of the gospel were moved by their sensitive concern for the welfare of the underprivileged to adopt a socialist point of view. We can find this represented in Franklin Monroe Sprague's *Socialism from Genesis to Revelation*, the work of a Congregationalist minister in Massachusetts published in 1893. We can find it in the labors of W. P. D. Bliss, another minister, who in 1889 became the editor of a periodical known as *The Dawn*, devoted to a kind of Fabianism. We can find it again in the labors of George D. Herron, a third clergyman, whose *Christian Society* was published in 1894 and who in the same year became one of the editors of a magazine called *The Kingdom*, in which again the Christian Socialist view was expressed. And the history of the Socialist party is sprinkled with the names of many other members of the cloth. By 1908 it was estimated that there were at least three hundred such.

Two other personalities indicate still further the varied character of the socialist movement. One of these is Julius

A. Wayland, a Midwesterner who had managed to amass a modest fortune in the newspaper business and in land speculation and who came to socialism with very little acquaintance with European Marxists. Wayland began publishing a sheet called *The Coming Nation* in 1893, which was followed in 1895 by a paper called *The Appeal to Reason*. Wayland was hearty, blunt, and little concerned with doctrine. But he had a very deep interest in the cause of socialism, and he was undoubtedly one of its most effective advocates. His paper was widely read, and one issue of it, just before the election of 1900, reached the extraordinary circulation figure of 927,000.

Another significant figure was Eugene V. Debs. Debs, like the other people we have mentioned, was a native-born American and, like Wayland, a Midwesterner. He began his activities in the cause of social improvement as a worker in the Brotherhood of Locomotive Firemen. In 1893, convinced of the necessity of industrial unionism, Debs organized a new labor group, the American Railway Union, and won a big strike against the Great Northern in that same year. But in 1894 his participation in the Pullman strike of that year ended in his arrest and imprisonment and, so he at times claimed, in his conversion to socialism. By 1897 Debs was widely known, and he was one of the organizers in Chicago of the group known as the Social Democracy of America.

It is difficult to classify Debs exactly from the point of view of socialist theory. He was not an educated man, or in any sense a systematic thinker. His strength lay in his deep sincerity, in his obvious sympathy with the less fortunate, in the passion he could bring to the cause of the underprivileged. Those who knew him—even when they could not accept his views—found in him something very lovable. No other figure in the socialist movement commanded a wider affection.

There were other strains in American socialism. Alongside the indigenous elements there were, too, Marxists, such as the New York group in which Morris Hillquit was perhaps the most conspicuous figure, and Social Democrats in the German tradition, such as one of the stalwarts of the party, Victor Berger of Milwaukee. Many different elements combined in the setting up of the new Socialist party in 1901, when it was formally launched upon its career.

Before examining that career, however, it should be noted that a beginning had been made when Debs ran for president in 1900, as the nominee of what was called the Social Democratic party, itself composed of those who could no longer put up with the doctrinaire authoritarianism of De Leon. The results of this campaign were not impressive; the vote in the nation as a whole was less than 100,000. But the distribution of the vote gave some room for encouragement; in more than half of the states a start, at any rate, had been made. By 1901, then, there appeared something on which to build when the Socialist party was itself launched under that name.

In 1904 the new political organization polled more than 400,000 votes. In 1908 it polled almost the same number. But in 1912 the figure rose to almost 900,000, almost 5 per cent of the total vote cast. Moreover, in a little more than a decade, the party had, according to Professor Richard Hofstadter, elected more than 1,039 candidates to office, including 56 mayors, 160 councilmen, and 145 aldermen. It had also sent Victor Berger to Congress from the Milwaukee district. Its membership rolls in the fall of that year were over 127,000. Its party press numbered more than thirteen dailies, five of them in English, and over three hundred weeklies, five-sixths of them in English. Wayland's sheet, already mentioned, had attained a circulation of half a million. The optimists among the Socialists might well have regarded the future with enthusiasm.

But the brightness of the picture was not unrelieved. Factionalism is no new thing in American politics, and it had infected the Socialists fully as much as it did the older parties. It is difficult, and it would be futile, to attempt to describe in detail the many brawls that went on within the party organization. Some of them, as always in such imbroglios, were based on personal antagonisms, but, above and beyond these, there were deep divisions within the party itself. Though it would hardly be right to say that there was a revolutionary element amongst the Socialists, in the full sense of the word, there was a left wing that constantly gave trouble to the more moderate elements. When the International Workers of the World was organized in 1905, Debs and some of the other more radical Socialists attended the initial gathering; conversely, Big Bill Haywood, who was active in the I.W.W., was also a member of the Socialist party. And, though in a relatively short time the two movements were divorced from one another, there remained in the Socialist organization a fringe that gave great concern to the conservatives. There was dissension, too, with regard to the attitude to be taken toward the American Federation of Labor. To Debs this movement, founded as it was on craft unionism, was anathema. There were other prominent persons in the party, such, for example, as A. M. Simons, who believed that it was extremely imprudent and impracticable to ignore the labor organizations, which, whatever their faults and limitations, might provide a solid nucleus for development. There was much difference of opinion, also, over dogma. As we have already seen, American socialism was only partly Marxian. Victor Berger, the Milwaukee representative of socialism, prided himself on his freedom from Marxian doctrine and was perhaps the party's foremost apostle of gradualism. Such conflicts of views naturally impeded the growth of the new political organization to a very substantial degree.

The most interesting struggles within the party, among a host of disputes, are two that arose when affairs looked brightest. The first was the discussion over what was known as the antisabotage amendment in the convention of 1912. At that assemblage there was introduced a resolution which read, "Any member of the party who opposes political action, or advocates crime, sabotage or other methods of violence, as a weapon of the working class to aid in its emancipation shall be expelled from the party." This declaration, a part of the constitution of the party, passed by a vote of 191 to 90.

It is entirely probable that not all those who voted against it approved crime or violence; they may simply not have wanted to apply this kind of test to membership. But the episode illustrates all too well the difficulty the Socialists were having with their left wing.

The second episode in the factional struggles of the party at this time was the expulsion of Big Bill Haywood from his membership on the National Executive Committee. This was a direct result of the antisabotage amendment just alluded to, for Haywood was accused of having violated this provision. On a referendum he was displaced by a vote of more than two to one. But here again this attempt to assert party discipline, though by no means disastrous, was hardly a source of strength to the organization.

There were, however, deeper reasons why the party's vote declined after 1912. Between 1912 and 1916 the course of events was extremely unfavorable to the new doctrine. The reforming spirit, of which socialism was only one expression, was effectively represented by the Wilson administration in the first two years of office. But more important than this was the coming of the war in Europe. The war split the party in two. From the Marxian point of view the only possible way to judge the conflict in Europe was from the angle of "a plague on both your houses." It was easier in the years 1914–1916 to maintain this position in America, where there was no direct involvement, than on the other side of the Atlantic, where national safety and ordinary patriotism dictated a surrender of dogma to the exigencies of the time.

Throughout this period a substantial element of the American Socialists clung to the oversimplified—indeed, the incorrect—view of the conflict, that only rival capitalist interests were involved and that the only thing for the United States to do was to steer clear of foreign entanglement. But this view of the matter was not held by all of the members of the party. There was a minority, and a powerful one, that believed that the cause of the Allies was the cause of righteousness and that dreaded a possible German victory as a threat to this country. Such persons could hardly have been edified by the platform adopted in the convention of 1916, calling for the immediate repeal of all laws for the increase of the military and naval forces of the United States, for the curtailment of the power of the President, for a national referendum as a condition precedent to any declaration of war, and for the abandonment of the Monroe Doctrine. Conversely, it may be assumed that some antiwar Socialists left their party to vote for Woodrow Wilson on the ground that, up to 1916, he had kept us out of war. The result was a very decided slump in the party vote in 1916. Allen Benson, a newspaper editor who carried the banner that year, made a miserable run, and the vote was cut by more than a third. True, the effects on the party did not immediately appear to be unfortunate. With American entry into the conflict, the Socialist organization attracted to itself many of those who resented the participation of the United States in the struggle against Germany. The arrest and conviction of Debs under the Sedition Act created an aura of martyrdom about the person of the Socialist leader. The Socialist ticket polled a very large vote when Morris Hillquit ran for mayor of New York in 1917. Party membership in the country at large, though dropping off slightly, by no means suffered a spectacular decline, and it was to rise again after the end of the war. When Debs ran from his prison cell for the presidency in 1920, he polled the largest vote he had ever polled—a little over a million, though percentagewise his showing did not compare with that of 1912.

But there is no doubt that the party was shaken by the war in influence, if not in numbers. Its press was demoralized. *The Appeal to Reason* came under new editorship, and that editorship supported the conflict. Some of the more conservative elements in the Socialist ranks began to think more seriously than before of alliances with other progressive groups. And the indigenous elements in the Socialist movement began to lose ground as well as to fall away.

The change in the composition of the party was affected not only by the war but also by the momentous event that had taken place in Russia. The Bolshevik revolution of 1917 created a very difficult situation for the American Socialists. The internecine strife that followed dealt a body blow to party unity. In the main, in the Socialist organization itself, by hook or by crook, the conservatives predominated. The party convention held in August 1919 defeated left-wing groups by a vote of considerably more than two to one. But the secessions that followed, the organization of the Communist party, and the reappearance of a Communist Labor party, all indicated that the movement was hopelessly split between the radicals and the moderates. The Socialist party was never again to attain the relative position that it had reached in the bright days before the war and the Bolshevik revolution.

In the period after 1920 the party organization declined very substantially indeed. In 1924 there was no separate ticket in the field, but a coalition was effected with other political groups in support of the candidacy of Senator Robert La Follette of Wisconsin. Senator La Follette polled a surprisingly large vote, 17.5 per cent of the total, and carried his own state of Wisconsin. But it is hard to see that the Socialist party benefited in any way by his candidacy. One of the most careful students of the subject, Professor David Shannon, believes that it came out of the campaign weaker than ever. Nor were there many signs of returning vitality in the years that followed. The country was enjoying extraordinary prosperity. In the elections of 1928 the Socialist vote, under a new leader, Norman Thomas (Debs had died in 1926), shrank to less than 300,000, less than Debs had polled in a much smaller total popular vote in 1904 and 1908. The actual membership of the party in that year was under eight thousand, and of these nearly half were now in the foreign-language affiliated organizations.

There was, it is true, a measure of Socialist revival in the period of the depression. As the situation became gloomier and gloomier and as the inadequacy of governmental measures to cope with it became more and more obvious, there was a substantial upturn. Under a vigorous party secretary many new locals were organized, and membership took a sharp upward turn. The intellectuals were again attracted toward the party by the leadership of Norman Thomas, and the roster of those who supported the Socialist ticket in 1932 is really quite impressive, with such names as Paul Douglas, John Dewey, Reinhold Niebuhr, Elmer Davis, and many others. In the election that year the Socialist vote again reached the neighborhood of a million.

But this was no more than a flash in the pan. By 1936 the vote had plummeted to 187,000. It went still lower in 1940, when it was only 99,000, and it surely was not helped at this time by the militantly antiwar stand of its candidate. It was down still further in 1944, and it recovered to only a little more than 130,000 in 1948. There could be no question that the party was dying. Thomas himself was thoroughly discouraged and urged that no candidate be nominated in 1952. His advice was not taken, and the candidate who did run, Darlington Hoopes, polled the abysmally low figure of 20,000 votes in the nation as a whole. In 1960 and 1964 the Socialist party disappeared from the ballot, so far as the national elections were concerned, and it is not likely to be revived.

Such is the story of the rise and fall of American socialism. It now remains to ask ourselves what were the reasons why the Socialist party had so brief an existence in

America and what were its positive contributions to American life.

We shall be better able to put the first of these questions in perspective if we recognize the fact that socialism strictly defined, that is, the operation of the instruments of production by the public authorities, has never won the support of any people who have been attached to the democratic way of life. There have been in the different countries of Europe varying degrees of state ownership of industry. The operation of railroads, for example, has been common. The control of electric power resources has often been put in the hands of government. The British have a publicly administered radio and at one time extended the socialist principle to the steel industry. But there is *no* democratically organized state, let us repeat, which has suppressed private enterprise for all forms of economic activity. The question of what should be taken out of the hands of the private capitalist has always been one of degree, never one of abstract principle.

We may go further. The popularity of the nationalization of industry in Europe has been declining. Actual experience with socialization in Britain has not won friends or influenced people. The socialist parties in the Scandinavian countries do not appear at all anxious to extend government operation in new areas. They stress, not so much socialism, as social justice, greater recognition of the role of the worker rather than a complete reorganization of the industrial system. Other examples of the same principle might be cited. In a sense, then, socialism has been declining in significance for some time not only in the United States but on the other side of the Atlantic.

Yet the fact remains that the role of socialism in the United States, as compared with the role of socialism in Europe, has been a comparatively insignificant one. The Socialist party, as we have seen, reached its apogee as far back as 1912. At the very bottom of the depression it was not so powerful as it had been twenty years before. And its diminishing vitality has not been at all matched, so far as the scale is concerned, by the decline of the socialist parties in Europe, more and more conservative though some of them have become. What, then, is the explanation of the peculiarly restricted role which socialism has played in the United States?

The answer to this question is to be found both in the character of American life and in the particular circumstances which conditioned our political development.

One of the most striking characteristics of the American people is their highly empirical view of the problems of society. The theoretical and the schematic rarely attracts our citizens. The role of the United States in the field of political abstraction has never been a very impressive one. Our most famous piece of political writing, the *Federalist Papers*, was intended to deal with a highly immediate situation and is by no means speculative in tone. Not only do our political parties have no clear body of doctrine, but Americans obviously prefer that they should not. The words "Republican" and "Democratic" cover a variety of views from the left to the right; they contain no clear and coherent philosophical implication, though sometimes an effort is made to produce a contrary impression. And, though there are political thinkers in America who have wished to see a reconstitution of American political parties along defined lines of "liberalism" or "conservatism," no such realignment has ever taken place, nor is there any likelihood that it will take place in the immediate future. It certainly runs counter to the mores of our professional politicians, whose understandable object in an election year is often to blur rather than to sharpen the issues in an effort to collect the maximum number of votes. On some specific question the political parties may take a fairly clear and unequivocal stand, the Republicans on the extension of slavery in 1860, on the gold standard in 1896, the Democrats on the League in 1920. But this is a very different thing from evolving a politico-economic philosophy from which deviation is deemed to be impossible.

There is another reason for the failure of socialism which is inherent in the American political system. The presidential system is highly unfavorable to the growth of *any* third party. The control of the presidential office is essential to the success of any political organization, at any rate in the long run. The more governmental activity is centered in Washington (and the tendency is in that direction) the truer this is. The two major parties are organized on a national scale; they also control the offices in the states; and to displace them is a truly Sisyphean labor, involving organization, funds, and activity on a colossal scale. Furthermore, they have been quick, either one of them or both of them, to recognize concrete grievances as they arise; and in this way an ambitious third-party group is likely to be deprived of nourishment. There was truth, as well as wisdom, in the remark of an eminent student of American politics when he declared many years ago that, if the American people wanted socialism, the Republican party would give it to them. The fact is they have never wanted it, but of that more a little later.

A third factor in the American scene that is of great significance is something already alluded to in a different connection, the long-time overweighting of the agrarian interests in the political organization of the United States. While, of course, the principle of government production may be extended to agriculture as well as to industry, the organization of the farmer as the servant of the state has in no country been easy. Even in a totalitarian country like the Soviet Union the collectivization of the farms has created the gravest problems and remains one of the most difficult questions that the Kremlin has to face. While the farmer in the United States has often manifested hostility to big business and has not objected to measures of governmental control directed against great combinations of capital, he has usually looked to more immediate remedies for his own difficulties, one of the most characteristic of these being some form of tinkering with the currency. His interest, in times of depression, has been in some immediate cure for his woes, not in sweeping theory which runs counter to his sturdy individualism and which, carried to its logical extreme, implies that *he* will be controlled as well as others. There have been, it is true, some instances of socialism in agrarian areas; we might have mentioned that the Socialist party was strong in Oklahoma in the first decade of the twentieth century. But it is significant that when, in some of the grain states, a program was put forward that involved an extension of state participation in industrial enterprise its founders carefully avoided the term "socialism" and called their organization by the nondoctrinal name of the Non-Partisan League.

Still another point may be made, and one of capital importance. Socialism in every country has had the overtones of the class struggle, which was central to Marxist theory. Sometimes the language in which this struggle was described has been violent, and sometimes it has been more restrained. But the centrality of the class struggle is alien to American experience. There is no country in the world where it has a more limited appeal. The Marxian doctrine that the rich constantly get richer while the poor constantly get poorer has certainly been far from sustained by the facts of American life. In this happy country of ours there has been the development of great wealth. But there has also been a rise in the standard of living of the less fortunate, a rise in which not all persons have participated but in which so many have had a share as to limit the appeal of the hypothesis we have been talking about. America has been the land of the middle classes, as I have already indicated in an earlier lecture. It has been the land of social fluidity and of individual opportunity. And a society which offers so great a reward to individual capacity and in which it is so easy—relatively speaking, at any rate—to move out of one economic group into another is not a society in which the gospel of socialism is likely to take deep root.

The matter can be put a little differently. Any economic order is likely to be judged, especially by so practical a people as the Americans, by its results. Without being in any way complacent about the American economic scene, recalling the swings of the business cycle and the suffering that they have entailed, recognizing the existence, even today, of depressed economic groups, one still sees that by the standard of actual accomplishment the American economy can hardly be regarded as a failure. To desire to make it over completely in the interests of a new doctrine has not therefore, been the natural American reaction to the problems that they have had to face.

The reasons just given for the limited success of the Socialist movement are related to the general atmosphere of the United States. But there is another set of reasons which are somewhat more specific in character. The first of these is the almost inevitable ambivalence inherent in socialism, as it has appeared in the Western world. On the one hand, the lingo has often been revolutionary; on the other hand, the practice has been cautious. There has at one and the same time been a doctrine and an immediate program. It has been difficult to unite under one party roof those whose ardor excels their discretion with the prudent advocates of a new gospel, or those who wish to see an ambitious and sweeping program with those who look to gradual change. As we have observed, there is factionalism in all political parties, but it is perhaps fair to say that factionalism among the Socialists exceeds anything yet seen in the older and more traditional party organizations.

This problem of ambivalence has been immensely sharpened by the advent of communism, and in the United States, as indeed in Europe, the socialist parties never recovered from the blow. For the advent of Bolshevism, as we have seen, posed a fundamental question which might be answered in either one of two ways. Was the socialist order so important to the world that it was worth sacrificing democratic values to attain economic bliss, or was it imperative to preserve the great libertarian ideals even if the day of the new economic order was long postponed? The ambivalence shows up, to give only one example, in Eugene V. Debs, who seemed to think that it was all right for the Moscow regime to limit freedom of speech since this was in the interest of the mass of the community. It created an inner turmoil in many Socialists which it was not easy for them to resolve.

At the same time the rise of Bolshevism discredited the Marxian ideal in many minds. The identification of the coming of the socialist state with violence repelled many people who might, under other circumstances, have been attracted to a socialist order.

There is another aspect of the matter that deserves particular attention. The Socialist party in the United

States has never succeeded in winning the allegiance of organized labor. The American labor movement at the end of the nineteenth and the beginning of the twentieth century was tightly tied to a somewhat narrow craft unionism, of which Samuel Gompers was the prototype and leader. There were occasions when the unions flirted with socialism; there was a mighty battle in 1893 in the American Federation of Labor convention when a plank calling for the "collective ownership by the people of all means of production and distribution" was actually adopted, though under circumstances which deprived it of some of its force. But this declaration was eliminated from the resolutions adopted in 1894, and, as Gompers' ascendancy in the union movement became more and more solid, the Socialist really had little chance. There was another flurry in 1902, a year in which Socialist influence in the unions may have reached its peak. But the lines held firm, and after that date it had become clear that the cause had little hope from the ranks of the A.F.L. Thus the source of much of the strength of the movement in other lands dried up in the United States.

Socialism never managed to win and *retain* the loyalty and enthusiasm of the American intellectuals. There was a time when it seemed as if very substantial headway was being made. The Intercollegiate Socialist Society, the brainchild of Upton Sinclair, though growing slowly at first, attained a very considerable significance in the days before World War I. There are many famous names in the ranks of its members, such as John Dewey, Paul H. Douglas, Florence Kelley, Harry Overstreet, and Ernest

Poole. But this group fell away in a very large degree in the period of World War I. The war became for a little while a great crusade, in very truth a crusade followed by disillusionment, but a crusade nonetheless. Among the men who left the party in 1917 were such individuals as William English Walling, one of the most sophisticated leaders of the party, John Spargo, who was the editor of an important Socialist paper and as influential on the right as Walling was on the left, Allen Benson, the party's presidential candidate in 1916, and such important literary figures as Upton Sinclair and Jack London. National feeling proved stronger than Marxian doctrine, and those who left at this time never returned.

But there is a bigger fact still. The truth of the matter is that many of those who voted the Socialist ticket were expressing a somewhat diffuse discontent with things as they were rather than subscribing to any dogma. The consequence is that socialism could not stand up against that moderate type of reform which has been characteristic of American politics. Let us look for a moment at the elections from this point of view. In 1904, after the country had savored the moderate liberalism of Theodore Roosevelt, the Socialist vote made almost no gain over 1900. It went up to 900,000 in 1912, a year of great political excitement and desire for social improvement, but Wilsonian progressivism followed and the vote shrank to 585,000 in 1916. The great depression year of 1932 saw the vote swell to 884,000; but the New Deal eviscerated the Socialist movement, and the vote in 1936 was a pitiful 187,000. There could be no clearer proof of the fact that the Socialist party vote was in substantial part a protest vote and that projects of reform operated almost invariably to bring many voters back to the ranks of the older parties.

Finally, the Socialist party never developed a great leader. There was, no doubt, a kind of charm about Eugene V. Debs; but Debs had neither the intellectual power nor the command over men which might have made him a really impressive figure. There have been few Americans more worthy of respect than Norman Thomas, but Thomas again lacked the qualities of personal leadership. Courageous, the sturdy champion of many a good minority cause, eloquent in his way, Thomas was too intellectual and too theological to become a master politician. He ran for the presidency five times. But he never touched deeply those elements in the community which might have rallied to socialist doctrine; he won widespread respect but not votes on any large scale; and his last years in politics were years in which he frankly confessed his own frustration.

But in analyzing the causes for the decline of socialism in the United States we are in danger of forgetting the positive contributions of the movement to American political and social progress. We cannot assign to the Socialists anything like the sole credit for the increasing sensitivity of Americans to the limitations of their economic order; but we must consider them as we consider other groups with impracticable and inacceptable programs, as useful gadflies and critics. And their role in this regard, though difficult to measure, was not without some

effect. First, the Socialists in their various party platforms became again and again the advocates of reforms
that were taken over and adopted by the traditional
parties. For example, the platform of 1904 called for
"the reduction of the hours of labor in proportion to the
increasing facilities of production," for "national insurance of working people against accidents, lack of em-
ployment, and want in old age," and "equal civic and
political rights for men and women." The platform of
1908 called for the abolition of child labor and for
graduated inheritance and income taxes, and for more
national concern with education. The platform of 1912
called for a minimum wage. But it is not necessary to go
further. We have said enough to illustrate the point that
the demand for reforms now generally accepted was
often voiced by the Socialists. True, this demand was
not voiced by them alone, and many less acceptable proposals were also put forward. But we cannot put aside
completely the influence of these men of the left on the
politics of their time.

In the second place, the ideology of socialism, false as
most Americans deem it, is in one respect worthy of
esteem. We do not need socialism in this country, in my
opinion, but we *do* need the social spirit, the spirit that
lays the emphasis on the well-being of society and not
on the acquisitive instincts of the individual. Let us admit
that good may come out of individual selfishness, that
many benefits are conferred upon the social body by men
who have no particular desire to serve a social end but
who by ability and force of character sometimes accom-

plish more than the idealists. Yet it remains true that insofar as socialism inculcates concern for the well-being of the mass, so far as it rises above a narrow class sectarianism and emphasizes the interests of the whole, it has been a healthful influence.

Thirdly, and most important of all, socialism raises a question that must be asked and that we cannot answer by some theoretical insistence on an individualistic philosophy. What is the proper role for the state to play? What are the proper activities for the state to pursue? Where do we draw the line between private and public enterprise? In closing this essay, I wish to address myself to this vital question.

Certainly the most doctrinaire friend of "free enterprise" will be ready to admit that there are some things the state should do. Few people get themselves into a passion over governmental operation of the postal system. There was a time when public education was denounced as an undue extension of public activity; it would be a very small minority that would take that position today. We are not, most of us, particularly shocked by municipal waterworks or gasworks. We bear with equanimity the idea of governmental control of credit through a governmental agency, the Federal Reserve Board. Obviously, there are some things today that most of us agree that government should do, and the practical question is, where do we wish to draw the line? In discussing this question, let it be clear that I am not talking about governmental *control*. I am discussing the actual operation by public authority of this or that economic activity. Are there any criteria by which we can determine whether, in a given case, state operation of industry is desirable? In considering this matter, I should like to broaden the frame of reference a little and draw some of my examples from the experience of countries other than the United States.

First, then, I should say that public operation might be rendered necessary when there exists a chronic state of hostility between the capitalist and the worker and when, in addition, the capitalist class is reluctant to abandon obsolete methods and bring the conduct of its industry up to date. The socialization or nationalization of the coal mines in Great Britain is a case in point. Not that the results achieved by the shift have been precisely sensational or have introduced a millennium into the coal industry. But in the situation that that industry faced, a change became inevitable, and this was recognized by many people who were far from doctrinaire Socialists and, indeed, by many who called themselves Conservatives. If the day ever comes when some industry in the United States proves itself incompetent to maintain a reasonable working relationship between labor and capital and to undertake necessary measures of advancement, we can be pretty sure that a demand for state operation will arise.

But more important than this is the case in which a tremendous capital investment is required which is beyond either the scope or the vision of the private entrepreneur. There have been striking examples of this in the recent history of the United States. The earliest of these

is, of course, the Tennessee Valley Authority. The critics
of T.V.A. are apt to lay the emphasis on the matter of
bookkeeping in relation to its operations in the field of
power. But this is hardly the heart of the matter. The
Tennessee Valley Authority has been a great experiment
in social planning and has rehabilitated and invigorated a
whole area. It ought to be looked at from this point of
view. Something of the same thing can be said of Bonne-
ville and Grand Coulee, and the same issue was involved
in the dispute over Hell's Canyon, where the opponents
of the concession made to private industry argued that a
low-level dam was inadequate and that only a high-level
dam, such as only government would be likely to finance,
was the true answer to the problem.

A still more striking example of the role of government comes in connection with the manufacture of the
atomic bomb. An investment of over two billion dollars
was involved here, and the very life of the nation may
have depended on that investment's being made. It had
to be made by government, and the results were brilliantly successful. It remains to be seen whether the private entrepreneur will assume the hazards, and undertake
the burdens, necessary for the further development of
atomic energy in the interests of peace.

To call the measures just cited "socialistic" is to con-
fuse rather than to illuminate the problem. There may
be cases in the future, as there have been cases in the
past, where government initiative in the sphere usually
reserved to private business will prove to be expedient.
But of one thing we may be sure. The sphere will always

be a restricted one. The acceptance of socialist *principle* has never been more remote than it is today. And this brings us to the central question to which the four preceding topics naturally lead. What is the American way of life? To what is America dedicated? This question I shall try to answer in the next essay.

The American Way

WE HAVE now examined American conservatism, American liberalism, and American radicalism. In the last of these essays on the American attitude toward political and economic problems, I propose to examine "the American way of life" as it is revealed in the action of the nation today. I shall do so in a spirit of appreciation of the many things of which we may be proud, but I shall naturally bear in mind the fact that our society is very far from perfect. We should at all times avoid the vice of self-complacency. We should remember that there are in this nation in the neighborhood of two million farm families living in squalor; that we still have noisome slums in our cities; that we still fail to give to our colored population the rights which it ought to enjoy; that our politics are far from those of the ideal state, with a disturbing amount of actual corruption and with much narrowness and much equivocation; that a portion of our business class is still living in a past that will never return; that a portion of our working class belongs to unions which are far too autocratically run, and a few of which are actually in the control of sinister forces; that we are by no means sure as yet that we have mastered the art of wise management of the national economy. Nevertheless, I think that by the comparative historical standard we may pronounce our society to be a good society.

The first thing to emphasize is the libertarian spirit that still exists in America. Over twenty years ago Sinclair Lewis wrote a much-read book, *It Can't Happen Here*, the thesis of which was that fascism might come to America. The cynical Huey Long suggested the same thing, though he said that it would come under the guise of antifascism. I believe nothing of the kind. I believe that the American system has many safeguards against the all-embracing state and that, so far as we can foresee the future at all, we can predict that in the future as in the past the spirit of liberty will flourish in this land.

In saying this, I am well aware that the tendency of American development is to enlarge the power of the federal government. This tendency has existed for some time and has been made necessary by the increasing complexity of our society and by the fact that truly national interests must be dealt with by the national authority. But there are built-in safeguards against the transfer of anything like total power to Washington, and these safeguards are as real today as they were fifty years ago.

One of these safeguards lies in the fact that it is practically impossible for a political party to perpetuate itself in power and to establish itself securely in a position of undisputed domination. The longest stretch of domination by one of our two political parties is that of the

Republicans from 1860 to 1884. But most historians believe that the Republican party was really defeated in 1876 and that the decision of the Electoral Commission in this disputed election was wrong. By 1880 only about seven thousand votes in the nation at large separated the Republicans from their rivals. The Democratic party was in power from 1932 to 1952, and the cynics were saying that its policy of handouts and of special favors to labor and to farmers might make impossible its dislodgement. The dislodgement came, nonetheless. There was a healthy reaction against the long tenure of the Democrats.

This reaction is partly a matter of the temper of the American people themselves, but it is immensely assisted by our federal system. No sooner is one party defeated at the federal level than it begins to build itself up in the states. The rehabilitation of the defeated political organization may be slow or fast, but it invariably takes place, and it is a useful and praiseworthy process. It makes one-party government of the kind that takes place in totalitarian states almost impossible.

We should remember, too, that the process of centralization in Washington has by no means been unqualified. Education, for example—a vital function if ever there was one—remains in the hands of the states, and the federal role, though increasing, can hardly be said to menace the freedom of instruction. It would be a very difficult thing to establish thought control in the United States. And such matters as social security, which are in part dealt with by national legislation, are in important respects still under state direction. The exact terms under which unemployment insurance shall be granted and the length of time the benefits shall last are not determined in Washington. To cite another example, under the Taft-Hartley Law the question of the legality of the union shop is left to state decision. Many other cases could be cited of the distribution of function between the state and the federal government. Thus gigantism in our system has been avoided.

But one can go farther than this. The checks on the executive under our system of government, and thus on the tendency toward autocracy, are many and various. There is a strong tradition of congressional independence, and it may be said that it is only at rare intervals and under very special conditions, such, for example, as those of the first years of the Wilson administration or the first years of the New Deal, that the executive comes anywhere near to dominating the legislative process. Franklin Roosevelt, after the greatest electoral triumph in American history in 1936, soon found himself at odds with the Congress and got very little of what he desired from the sessions of 1937 and 1938. The immense personal prestige of President Eisenhower by no means meant that the legislators acted as his docile instrument.

One of the signs of congressional independence is the legislative investigation. With painful memories of the McCarthy period not so far behind us, we shall many of us agree that this power of investigation can be and has been shamefully abused. But on the whole it is a healthy thing that the national legislature is able to be critical of the executive and exercise a watchful supervision over the legislative process. There are many investigations that do good, the investigation of the twenties, for example, that led to the exposure of the oil scandals, the investigation *of* McCarthy, not *by* him, that exposed the Senator to the just contempt of a large body of public opinion.

The jealousy of executive influence has been expressed in striking fashion in the anti-third-term amendment to the Constitution and in the efforts of Senator Bricker in the early fifties to limit the treaty-making power of the executive. I do not intend to examine either of these matters in detail, and I do not wish to be understood as endorsing the limitation on the number of presidential terms or the restrictionist notions of the Senator from Ohio. But proposals of this kind reveal a distrust of executive power that is, in its general aspects, by no means entirely unhealthy.

Furthermore, we have the courts. We cannot foresee the future, but there have certainly been—and are today —many occasions when our judicial tribunals stand in the way of the abuse of power, either by the executive or by the national legislature. The invalidation of the National Industrial Recovery Act by a unanimous bench in 1935 was a fundamental judicial declaration against the undue concentration of power in Washington. The decision in the Humphreys case dealt a body blow to a highly popular and successful President when he attempted to exceed his authority in the removal of a member of an independent administrative commission.

The abuse of power by the McCarthy committee was in 1956 censured by the courts, which have found that that committee exceeded its authority. The problem of security in government has been given a new perspective by a judicial decision that it is only in sensitive areas that removal on security grounds ought to be permitted. This is not to say that in times of great popular excitement the courts may not go astray. But it is certain that in our judicial system we have one important safeguard against the tyranny of the executive or the passions of the hour.

Finally, we may, on the basis of the record, trust the sobriety of the American people. They can be and have been led astray; they have not always exhibited their best qualities in dealing with their problems; but they are ready to react strongly against the excessive use of authority, as their attitude toward the Eighteenth Amendment might well be used to prove.

The prejudice which Americans feel against the undue concentration of political power is equally present when it comes to economic matters. From a very early day the undue concentration of economic power has awakened antagonism in the United States. There are two sides to President Andrew Jackson's famous struggle with the Second Bank of the United States; but the President's distrust of a financial institution which wielded, in its own day, an enormous power over the credit system of the country was typical of a very wide body of opinion and thoroughly characteristic of the attitude of the average American. A much longer struggle, but in the end one which had substantial results, was the struggle against monopoly and for the regulation of industries affected with a public interest. Let us look first for a moment at the Sherman Antitrust Law. Passed in 1890, it was for a few years largely ineffectual. But it was invigorated by the administration of Theodore Roosevelt, and it has played a substantial part in the development of our economic order. Of course it has not prevented a strong tendency toward oligopoly in American economic life, but it has been certainly something of a curb on ruthless business practice on the part of powerful economic units. What the American people think of concentration of economic power is also illustrated by the unpopularity of the National Industrial Recovery Act. This statute, in practice, gave to the more powerful business concerns a dominating role in the conduct of each individual industry, and it awakened wide resentment among the small business men. It was virtually collapsing when the Supreme Court declared the law unconstitutional.

As for the principle of regulation, we have seen it constantly gaining ground in American life. As early as the 1870's the states began to attempt to regulate the railroad industry, the colossus of those days, and the first federal statute was enacted in 1887. In its initial years federal regulation of railroads proved to be largely ineffectual, and it was much impeded by the conservatism of the courts. But by 1906 new legislation strengthened the position of the government, and subsequent statutes brought the rail system of the country under firm federal control. In the same period the regulation of public utilities became a reality. The first important statutes were enacted in Wisconsin and New York, and the latter of these owes much to the pertinacity and ability of Charles Evans Hughes. This pioneer legislation was widely imitated, and the principle of the control of public utilities has now been accepted throughout the country. In due course we have carried this principle further. We have, now for twenty years, regulated the stock market; we have a national statute dealing with the electric power industry; and the courts have sanctioned a large number of state statutes by which the area of regulation has been widely extended.

Or take another aspect of the question, the control of credit. In the complex economy of the twentieth century it has become clearer and clearer that the right to grant or withhold credit, and especially the right to fix the terms of credit, is a matter of transcendent importance. Since 1913 we have had in the Federal Reserve Board an agency which deals with this matter, and the Board's authority has been widened and strengthened by the legislation of 1933 and 1935. What used to be called "the money power" has been brought under public control.

But if the American people have not wished to see an undue concentration of power in the hands of the capitalist, so they have not wished to see an undue extension of the influence of any other economic group. Without endorsing that complicated statute, the Taft-Hartley Law, which contains so many provisions that a generalized judgment on it is extremely dangerous, it is an interesting commentary on the American temper that, when a feeling arose that the labor unions were coming to exercise their power in an extreme way, it was easy to get through Congress legislation aimed at redressing the balance, legislation which was enacted over the veto of the President. There have been signs of a similar tendency so far as agriculture is concerned. The legislation of the thirties for the relief of the farmer was widely accepted. But of late the feeling has grown up that the principle of parity payments has been carried too far and that it needs correction. And, though no essential change of the system has been made, this point of view has found increasing expression.

The matter can be put in another way. To doctrinaire critics of the capitalist system, the structure of the American economy is monolithic in character. Of course it is really nothing of the kind. Just as there exist many checks in our political system, intended to prevent the growth of arbitrary power, so there exist checks in our economic system. Professor J. Kenneth Galbraith has put the matter brilliantly in his little book, *The American Economy*. The power of business is balanced by the power of labor and of the agrarian interests. The power of the great magnates in the business field is limited, at least in some degree, by the power of the small business men. The interest of one sizable business group is balanced by that of another group, as, for example, in the struggle that goes on between those who desire protection for their industry and those who wish lower tariffs and the opening of foreign markets. Thus there are many safeguards against that abuse of economic power which, if it occurred, would be as intolerable as the abuse of political power would be. There is a federal system in the economic world, as there is a federal system in the world of politics.

If the forces that make for freedom as against authority are strong in the world of government and of economics, so they are strong, too, in the religious and intellectual sphere. The diversity of religious life is one of the most extraordinary features of the American scene. In no country that I know are there so many sects, each independent of all others. In none would there be greater sensitiveness to the threat of domination by any single religious group. There are parts of the world where a single church is entrenched in power in a way that cramps not only liberty but progress. No such danger is to be apprehended in the United States.

Nor need we, viewing the matter broadly, fear for intellectual freedom in the United States. This is not to say that there is not a certain pressure for conformity. It is not to say that there are not more cases than we would like to think of interference with the liberty of instruction in schools and colleges. But we have to view the record in the large. The great universities of the country have an honorable devotion to academic freedom. They not only exemplify but they foster it. If heterodoxy of an extreme kind is rare in our schools, it is certainly in large degree because it is rare in American life itself. There have been in the past—and there may be in the future—unhappy episodes in the field of American education. But I am sure that if you asked the thousands of teachers and professors in this country if they felt themselves coerced in opinion, or if they had in their own experience seen many instances of such coercion, they would respond in the negative. In this field we must not permit ourselves any undue complacency, but neither must we exaggerate the extent of interference with freedom of instruction.

Libertarianism then is the first constituent of the American way. The second, as I see it, is empiricism. This is to be seen in both our political and economic life. To take the political side of things first, Americans will put up with any illogicality in politics so long as the practical consequences do not prove to be distasteful. Take, for example, such a thing as equal representation in the Senate of the United States. There can be no justification for it in theory. Why should Nevada, with something like 200,000 people, have the same weight in the Senate as New York, with something like thirteen million? Is not this the very negation of democracy? At first blush, it seems so. But almost fifty years ago Woodrow Wilson gave an answer to this question. It is that we secure in the Senate regional representation, as distinguished from represenation on the basis of population. And in a country as vast as the United States there is something to be said for this. Add that the small states have contributed at least their fair share of able and independent men to the national legislature and you have a practical justification of what can hardly be reconciled with abstract notions of democracy. Take the same problem in the state of New York. The great metropolis is egregiously underrepresented in the state legislature. But this under-representation works out practically well enough. It prevents the domination of the upstate citizens by the denizens of the great city. And, at the same time, since the party which is the strongest in the agrarian areas can succeed in politics only by winning the governorship, it must pay due heed to the point of view of the city population. The result has been very substantial and measured progress, despite the departure from the democratic ideal of equal representation.

I have already had a little to say about the role of our political parties. They are possibly the most unprincipled political organizations to be found in any one of the great democratic states. The party label covers a multitude of divergences. The isolationist and the friend of international co-operation, the contented conservative and the advocate of change, the friend of the farmer, the worker, and the businessman, all are to be found in both the great political organizations. No doubt the point can be exaggerated. The flavor of the Democratic party, despite the southern conservatives who act as a brake on its northern wing, is different from that of the Republican, which manages somehow or other to combine an especial concern for the business interests with sufficient attention to farmers and workers to win a good many state elections and at least a few national elections. But in both parties there is little insistence on any rigid set of principles. Rarely is the issue sharply joined between them. Whoever studies the history of the New Deal will discover that much of the legislation of that period was supported by a majority of the Republicans. Whoever examines the record of the Eisenhower administration will find that much of its support in the Congress came from the other side of the party aisle. Whoever examines the line-up of a few decades ago on such questions as immigration or prohibition will find that there was no division of party lines. American politicians are rarely tied to doctrine. They are looking for votes, and within certain bounds of scruple will take them where they find them. The result, as Herbert Agar, among others, has pointed out in especially stimulating fashion, is highly satisfactory in practice, however revolting to the devotees of principle. Though there is a certain amount of hypertension and partisan nonsense in an election year, there is none of that factional fury that makes the politics of some continental European states so bitter and often so ineffectual. The tendency toward the center, toward what will be accepted rather than what is right by some abstract standard, toward the reconciliation of interests rather than the sharpening of class and sectional antagonisms, has produced in practice a government which manages to unite order and progress to a high degree, which moves forward but rarely at a pace that calls for drastic measures of reaction, which maintains the social peace at the same time that it recognizes the necessity for new adjustments. This is the way Americans like it. They have viewed with scant interest the third parties that intrude upon the scene from time to time. When they vote for the candidates of these parties, they often do so, not with one or the other of the traditional parties into action. When the special grievance which calls forth the third-party vote is satisfied, or when circumstances make it less acute, the third-party voter returns to the fold of those all-embracing and catholic organizations which have room for the widest divergences of opinion.

The Americans have dealt in the same way with the problems of their economic life. In the expanding society of the nineteenth century, with its broad agrarian base and with its early-stage capitalism, they were ready to believe with Thomas Jefferson that that government was best which governs least. They acted on this theory because for a long time it worked, because it gave free scope to individual enterprise, permitted the settling of a continent, and produced a society which was, despite its defects, moving forward and not backward. No doubt they were devoted to this doctrine a little longer than was wise. While they began to be aware of the necessity of government controls in the latter part of the nineteenth century, while the first major steps to assert this control were taken in the administrations of Theodore Roosevelt and Woodrow Wilson, there was still much of the spirit of *laissez faire* in the years following the American victory in World War I. But with the coming of the Great Depression the scene changed, and in the last twenty years the American economic order has been refashioned to meet the needs of our own time.

This refashioning is connected with what is known as the New Deal. And, now that we have some historical perspective on the events of the 1930's, we can see that what was involved was adaptation, not revolution. The nature of our society has not been *fundamentally* changed. It still rests, as in the judgment of most of us it should rest, on a system of private enterprise; it still gives wide scope to the energy of the initiative of the individual; it is still, in the literal sense of the word, a society based on capitalism, as distinguished from socialism or any other "ism." What was done when the nation underwent a great depression, the most serious in its history, was not to overturn the existing structure but to revamp it. And the President who presided over the process was, by every test, an empiricist; some persons would call him an opportunist. It was characteristic of Franklin Roosevelt that he should think in terms of bold, persistent experimentation rather than of dogma; that he should compare himself to the quarterback of a football team who calls the plays as the occasion demands; that he should respond to a question as to his political faith that he was a Christian and a Democrat, two nouns which, whatever emotional response they may provoke, can hardly be described as embodying a fixed and definite program.

But let us look at the New Deal years in a little more detail. Take, for example, the banking crisis of 1933. A doctrinaire solution of the problem would have been the nationalization of the financial institutions of the country. What was done was to shore up the existing structure. Take the question of the revival of industry. What was done was not to socialize industry but to try an experiment in industrial self-government, the famous

N.I.R.A. Take the question of the currency. What was done was not to embark upon unlimited inflation but to devalue the dollar and to experiment with bidding up the price of gold. Take the question of agriculture. What was done was not to cut the farmer loose from his past but to experiment with various expedients for raising farm prices, and it may be added that we are still experimenting. In each of these cases the point does not lie in the success or the failure of the specific project. It lies, I repeat, in the highly nondoctrinal character of the approach.

What is equally significant in the New Deal period is the manner in which so much of the legislation was directed against specific abuses. In retrospect it seems almost incredible that so important an agency as the New York Stock Exchange was left almost entirely unregulated until 1933. It was only after the nation had suffered the bitterest of experiences through the drastic erosion of stock values, and only after grave abuses in the issuance of securities had been discovered, that measures of control were actually enacted. There is almost no one who would not say today that such measures were justified. In the same way the banking crisis led to measures of reform that have been generally applauded and that have stood the test of time. Social insurance had been adopted in almost all of the great nations of Europe. The enactment of the great program of social security that came to fruition in 1935 was merely a recognition of the lessons of experience. In the prevailing distress suffered by agriculture in the depression some kind of moratorium on farm indebtedness was a practical necessity. And, though the program of subsidies to agriculture has raised a good many questions and has left some of these questions unsolved, some emergency measures for the relief of the farmer were drastically needed when the Roosevelt administration took office. Finally, in an era of social discontent, a relief program adequate to deal with the existing situation, and administered by the federal government, was a necessary precaution against the growth of radicalism. The same thing is to be said with regard to the public works legislation of 1933.

In every one of these measures, what was done was done to meet an immediate situation, and each had its roots in the American past. Not one of them deserves to be described by the nasty word "socialism."

But the empirical nature of the New Deal was still better illustrated by the attitude assumed toward public finance. Orthodox economics, such as was advocated by President Herbert Hoover, called for the balancing of the federal budget, and Roosevelt himself, in a speech which he was later anxious to forget, had talked in these terms in the course of the 1932 campaign. Indeed, in the first days of the new administration the passage of the so-called Economy Act was a gesture in the direction of conventional finance. This policy was soon abandoned. But it was not abandoned on the basis of any fiscal theory. A new fiscal theory was evolved and gained considerable currency, and its most effective presentation will always be connected with the name of John Maynard Keynes. But the President, we repeat, was no theoretician; his enemies went so far as to tax him with a jaunty disregard of economic law. What he saw was merely a practical problem, the problem of relieving human suffering whether the budget was balanced or not. He simply put adequate relief to the unemployed ahead of any doctrine. He never committed himself to reckless finance of the inflationary variety. He vetoed a bonus bill in 1936 on grounds that might well have given satisfaction to economic conservatives. When it looked as if prosperity were returning in 1936 and early 1937, he made a new attempt to make financial ends meet, and it was only when the economic indicators turned down again that he reverted to deficit financing. He never gave up the idea of a balanced budget, though he was not to realize it in practice. His approach to the problem, let us repeat, was purely empirical.

It was the same way with the problems created by the war. The control of prices and wages was a necessary policy at a time of great governmental borrowing. Rationing followed as a necessary consequence. But, just as soon as the war was over, the country reverted (some people believe that it reverted too soon) toward an economy under less strict governmental control.

We have been talking of governmental policy. But what is fully as interesting as the New Deal policies is the position assumed by a group of progressive businessmen in the period since the war. The program of the Committee for Economic Development is no figment of an idealist imagination. It is no doctrinal approach to the problems of a more stable economic order. It represents the thinking of the more enlightened of the business class, and the chances are that it will play a very great part in the actual economic evolution of the future. This program therefore deserves analysis.

The first point to be noted is the federal control of the money supply. The principle is accepted that the machine of credit is too important to the economic health of the country to be left in private hands. The principal agency through which this machine is to be regulated is the Federal Reserve Board. In times of business optimism, the raising of interest rates is regarded as a means of preventing a speculative boom. In times of declining business, interest rates are to be lowered. One does not have to believe implicitly in the all-embracing effectiveness of such a mechanism to know that we have here a reasonable and useful means of giving a greater degree of stability to our economy. And, in practice, we have seen this machinery more and more effectively utilized. Since 1952 (and the fact should be noted that the change came before the end of the Truman administration) the Federal Reserve Board has been permitted to function independently, and the health of the economy has been considered to be more important than the financial pressures exerted on the Treasury of the United States. The results, so far at any rate, appear to have been happy ones. They involve a nonpolitical use of the money power, something to which the nation has come after a bitter experience both with the system of unregulated private credit and with the subservience of the banking system to the government itself. This is the practical way to deal with one of the largest of current economic problems, and it is thoroughly in the American temper.

Measures of this kind are conceived by the Committee on Economic Development as one of the means of strengthening the economic organism. There is also a fresh attitude toward the budget. In good times the budget is to be balanced. Obviously, reckless federal spending leads to inflation, and inflation, if not controlled, can lead to an unregulated boom. It is thought therefore to be the part of fiscal prudence to attempt to keep expenditures and income at about the same level in good times. Some people might argue that small deficits might be tolerated if prices were at the same time kept within bounds by a substantial increase in productivity. But fiscal caution when optimism reigns is the recommendation of the C.E.D.

On the other hand, the Committee has moved a long way from the theory, cherished so widely twenty years ago, that the proper policy in times of a business downswing is to increase taxes and balance the budget at all costs. According to its program, deficits are to be frankly accepted as desirable in a deflationary period, and a whole series of measures is projected to put more buying power in the hands of the public. For example, taxes may be reduced, and tax refunds and extension of tax carry-backs may be put into effect. Federal borrowing may be increased. A program of public works, planned in advance of the crisis, may be vigorously prosecuted. State and local governments may be assisted by grants of federal credit. The whole economy is to be stimulated into renewed activity by measures such as these. As to the efficacy of such a program, there may still be doubts in some quarters. But, if these steps are taken with reasonable promptitude, most persons believe, they may at least mitigate the violence of the oscillations to which business has been subject in the past.

But the program of the C.E.D. is by no means a program which puts all the emphasis on what government can do to avert a depression. It rests upon no such narrow basis of either theory or practice. A large part of its remarkable report of 1954 is concerned with the responsibilities of private enterprise, with such questions as the encouragement of technological research, with the improvement of marketing techniques, with the improvement of inventory policies, with the more effective planning of plant and equipment expenditures, and the like. The emphasis, in other words, is not concerned with abstractions but with the results of experience. Nothing could better illustrate the highly empirical character of the American mind than this program, drawn up by some of the leading businessmen of America and harmonizing the interests and activities of private enterprise and of the vast governmental machine.

Before leaving this subject of American empiricism, a word should be said about the new government agency set up since the end of the war, the Council of Economic Advisers. Here is an agency which is to watch over the economic trends and make recommendations for action as occasion arises. It proceeds on a short-term basis, studying and adjusting itself to events. In the technique which it employs, and in the attitude which it represents, it affords another evidence of the highly pragmatic way in which mid-twentieth-century America faces its current problems.

Libertarianism, empiricism, these are two of the outstanding characteristics of the American way. The third factor which ought to be mentioned is the faith of the Americans in the values of a fluid society. This is a matter which goes to the very heart of the American system.

In a sense, as I have already pointed out, American society has been fluid, as compared with that of Europe, from the beginning of its history. It is true that in colonial America there was an aristocratic class. There were the great slaveholders in the South, the patroons in the Hudson River valley, and the commercial bigwigs of New England. It is also true that the aristocratic tradition lasted into the nineteenth century, but the character of American life has not made for the growth of a hereditary moneyed class. There were, it is true, in the nineteenth century great accumulations in the hands of a few, and, in some cases, a small number of families have been able to retain and transmit wealth over a number of generations. But the character of American life has from the beginning made this difficult, and it is probably going to be more difficult rather than less so. In the nature of the case, a plutocracy is less able and less enduring than an aristocracy based upon the ownership of the soil. The management of business demands high qualities which are by no means always transmitted from father to son. The increasing complexity of American technology puts more and more power into the hands of the managerial class, and more and more leads to the divorce of ownership from management. Ownership itself becomes diffused, partly through heavy taxation, through both income and inheritance taxes, and partly through the natural tendency of the well-to-do to diversify their holdings. New opportunities constantly present themselves, not only to rise in the industrial hierarchy but to initiate new enterprises. The extraordinary inventiveness of the American people, and their restless interest in new gadgets of every kind, opens the way to new successes in the industrial field. A dynamic society, a society where energy flows from the mass, can hardly fail to be a fluid society.

The keystone, however, of the fluidity of American life lies in the American conception of education. Judged by the comparative standard, no nation comes anywhere near to educating so many of its young people at the college level as does the United States. In the college year 1963 the enrollment in liberal arts colleges and universities was over 3,000,000. If to this were to be added the enrollment in teachers' colleges, technological schools, and junior colleges, the number would be swelled by another 2,000,000. The number of undergraduate degrees conferred upon men alone in the year 1963 would be more than four times the number of persons enrolled in all the institutions of advanced learning in Great Britain. The number of persons in American institutions and colleges would be more than twenty times the number in

Great Britain. A ratio based on differences of population would be something like seven to one.

But it is not in numbers alone that the American educational system has a special place in the scheme of things. In such a country as Britain, a large proportion of college students are destined for the professions, for the law, for medicine, for the church, or possibly for a public career. In the United States, on the other hand, education has a much wider meaning and a deeper significance. Knowledge is conceived of not as polite learning or professional training in the narrow sense but as something that can be made valuable in a wide variety of callings. American schools of agriculture have a special place in the scheme of things. American schools of business education abound. Courses in home economics play a part in a very large number of American colleges. And all of these open the way to the earning of a living and possibly to emergence from one social class into another. This need to broaden instruction at the higher level seems likely to increase, for scientific methods are being applied to more and more aspects of life.

Just as we have given a larger meaning to education at the academic level, so we are attempting an enormous task in our secondary and elementary schools. And here again a comparison with Britain may be instructive. In this country about 40 per cent of our population is enrolled in the schools; in the British Isles the proportion is about 12.5 per cent. And as unskilled labor plays a diminishing role in our economy, education has an increasingly important part in preparing men and women who do not go to college for effective participation in the community and in helping them to improve their economic status.

It is true that in this area of the national life we face nothing less than a crisis. We have a great need for teachers, and this need will hardly be filled until we give to the teaching profession a position of greater prestige and greater reward than it offers today. Even so, the problem is enormous. It will call for high imagination, audacity in the application of new ideas, willingness to pay the price in the form of increased taxation and of increased private benevolence to our institutions of learning. But there are increasing signs of awareness of the problem, and, as the situation becomes more and more apparent, there is reason to believe that it will be met more forthrightly and more vigorously. The growing interest of the great corporations in education is one of the interesting signs of the times.

Surely nothing is more distinctive—and more American—than our educational system. Its preservation and extension is a public necessity. It is a necessity not only for maintaining our way of life but in the interests of the national security as well. We shall need to stimulate our whole population to technological and scientific advance as never before in the days ahead. Only if the careers open to talented people are recognized as a necessity can we hope to maintain our position in the world at large.

These are some of the thoughts that occur to me in the celebration of the American way. There are other ideas which I have not mentioned. The ethical tone of a society is patently of the first importance. The competitive spirit is significant. The problems of population and public health have much to do with the vitality and with the success of any nation. But on the three bases I have mentioned rests much of the success of this nation. So long as the libertarian spirit exists, so long as Americans retain their strong preference for what works as against some doctrine of what ought to work, so long as the sources of American vitality are refreshed and invigorated through our schools and our colleges, we need not fear for the future. Strong in our libertarian faith, practical as to means, ever watchful to prevent the stratification of our society, we hope to go forward in the American way. We can even hope that that way will be an example, an inspiration, and an encouragement to the rest of the world.